Introduction

The Unmarked Grave

ANY ENGLAND cricketer needing inspiration as he leaves the dressing room at Lord's to do battle might look up at the honours board he must pass. This monument to past feats on the most iconic ground in cricket celebrates those with Test centuries or five wickets in an innings. Should he or she glance up, the first very name on the board is E. Peate whose six Australian wickets in the 1884 Test started a tradition now copied at Test grounds across the world. Only the greatest cricketers in the land have access to this sanctum but we lesser mortals who fly into or out of Leeds-Bradford airport and look out of the window may spot, just a few yards from the runway, the neatly laid out headstones of Yeadon cemetery. There, in plot 214A, lies the body of that same E. Peate but, unlike at Lord's, there is no gilt inscription, no proclamation to the world of his achievements. For Edmund Peate – better known as Ted – lies in an unmarked grave. There is no headstone, no memorial, just a patch of bare grass to mark the passing of a man who was considered at the time to be the best spin bowler in the world.

Worse, those who do remember Ted Peate tend to remember him more for his fall from grace than for his fiendish bowling which left Victorian batsmen – foremost amongst them Australians – flummoxed. As the decades have passed, Peate has been vilified for his lifestyle as the story of his sacking drifts down the decades. To pick just two examples, the eminent author Simon Wilde in his book *England the Biography* states unequivocally that Peate was sacked for 'insobriety'. Derek Hodgson, in his *Official History of Yorkshire County Cricket Club* says he was disposed of because of a 'disorderly private life'. Even the 'Bible of Cricket', *Wisden*, tut-tuts. Its obituary of Peate says 'without using a harsh word it may fairly be said that he would have lasted longer if he had ordered his life more carefully'. More recently, *Wisden* seems to have a 'down' on Peate. Its 2011 collection of writings about Yorkshire County Cricket Club lists statistics on the club, including all those who have taken hat-tricks. They are all there, names like Trueman, Hirst and Verity, with one exception: inexplicably Peate's two hat-tricks in Yorkshire's history are omitted from the list.

The story of Peate's downfall while seemingly at the peak of his powers is too good to omit. It goes something like this: the Honourable Martin Bladen Hawke, upon his appointment as captain of Yorkshire, inherited a team of talented cricketers whose achievements were considerably less than the sum of their parts. He supposedly described them as 'ten drunks and a parson'. Notably ill-disciplined, they were all professionals from a working-class background who treated playing cricket for Yorkshire as a fun interlude between their evening drinking sessions. Hawke was determined to whip this collection of jack-the-lads into shape and was ruthless when he ran into any resistance to his new, disciplined regime. He shocked not just Yorkshire but the cricketing world when he dropped his side's most potent attacking force and told Peate that his services were no longer required. The first of the ten drunks had been made an example to the rest.

Ten Drunks
and a
Parson

IAN LOCKWOOD

Ten Drunks
and a
Parson

The Life and Times of

TED PEATE

First published by Pitch Publishing, 2025

Pitch Publishing
9 Donnington Park
85 Birdham Road
Chichester, West Sussex
PO20 7AJ
www.pitchpublishing.co.uk
info@pitchpublishing.co.uk

A CIP catalogue record is available for this book
from the British Library.

ISBN 978-1 80150 995 4

Printed and bound on FSC® certified paper in line with
our continuing commitment to ethical business practices,
sustainability and the environment.

Printed and bound in India by Replika Press Pvt. Ltd.

Contents

So the story goes. It is an irresistible tale but one which drowns Peate's exploits for Yorkshire and England. The alleged drunk played a pivotal role in perhaps the most famous Test match in history, the one which gave rise to the Ashes, when England, chasing a mere 85 in their second innings to win at The Oval in 1882, were bowled out for 77. The last wicket to fall was that of Peate. If anyone has heard of Peate's contribution to the game it usually is about him being sent in with instructions to play a straight bat, a Victorian equivalent to a Jack Leach role while at the other end Charles Studd would do the Ben Stokes heroics. Alas, Ted went for glory, missed the ball and was bowled, leading to the funereal description of the demise of English cricket, killed by Peate. His flippant comment that he couldn't trust Mr Studd to get the runs hardly helped his cause.

Yet in that same year of 1882, Peate took 214 first-class wickets. No-one had ever done better. The following season he took eight Surrey wickets for just five runs. The Australians grew sick of the sight of him. In one season he met them 14 times playing not just for Yorkshire and England but also for invitational sides such as The North or The Players. In 1887 an Ilkley publishing firm, Brumfitt and Kirby, produced a book called *England v Australia At the Wicket* which recorded all 11-a-side matches between English teams and Australia from 1862 including those not classed as Test matches. Peate topped the list of leading wicket-takers with 163 at an average of 14.1.

I first came across Ted Peate when I was researching a history of my home town of Skipton in North Yorkshire. Firmly believing that sport plays a vital role in the history of any community, I came across newspaper accounts that the former England and Yorkshire professional had signed to play for the Skipton club. He was to remain there for eight seasons until, in 1900, reports of his death were published. I confess that I had never heard of him. A quick trawl of the internet unearthed the superficial story of his life – how he had been sacked by Lord Hawke for being a drunk, how he had cost England the Ashes, how he had held for many years various Yorkshire bowling records and how he was buried in an unmarked grave in a public cemetery. There was no biography of him, no-one to put his side of the story. He was forever doomed to be the first of the 'ten drunks' to be forced out of the door. I went to the cemetery in Yeadon and stood on the blank piece of ground, surrounded by memorial stones to his contemporaries, Ted's bones beneath my feet. I studied again the studio portrait of him, doleful eyes staring out above his trademark moustache. I realised that posterity had dealt Ted a poor hand. It was time to tell his story.

Chapter 1

The Clown Cricketer

EDMUND PEATE, who would invariably be known by the name Ted, was born on 2 March 1855 in Holbeck. Situated south of the river Aire in Leeds, mid-19th-century Holbeck was heavily industrialised, the epitome of the smoky, northern working-class district thrown up to feed the factories of the Industrial Revolution. Row after row of crowded terraced houses were home to the factory- and mill-workers of south Leeds. Today, the houses are largely gone, replaced by industrial estates or the concrete of the M621 motorway which takes traffic out of Leeds and on to the M1 and M62. Peate's parents were employed in the textile trade. His father, David, described himself in the 1851 census as a clothier which covers a multitude of occupations but probably meant he and his family would be involved in the cutting, stitching and preparation of cloth, possibly at home, if not in a small workshop, which was sold on to larger merchants. David had married Mary Ann (sometimes spelt Marianne) in Guiseley in 1844. He had been born in the next village, Yeadon. This large village to the north of Leeds, situated cheek by jowl with Leeds-Bradford airport, was to play a significant role in Ted's life, drawing him and his family back there like a magnet.

David and Mary Ann already had three children when Ted was born – Ann, born in 1844, Edward, born in 1849 and Eliza born in 1852 and the 1861 census shows the family to be living at 4 New Inn Yard on Hunslet Road, a small house abutting the New Inn pub. Although the pub itself is still there (now a convenience store), the crowded houses accessed through a narrow passage leading into a dingy, dirty courtyard have been cleared. That 1861 census informs us that a fifth child, Sarah Maria, had been born and that David Peate had a new job. He describes himself as a stationary engine operator – in other words operating the steam engine which drives the machinery in a mill. However, David died in 1863. The same year the eldest child Ann moved out of the family home when she married Renwick Myers, of Yeadon, however, she died three years later. Ted was seven years old and his widowed mother was drawn back to her Yeadon roots. With her three children she moved in with her late husband's parents, Cain and Maria Peate whose address was The Green in Yeadon. We don't know what sort of education Ted had (although he was certainly able to read and write proficiently) but he would have been put to work as soon as possible. For the 1871 census, Cain was 65 and still working as a cloth weaver and he had managed to get Mary Ann, Ted (now aged 15) and Eliza (18) employment in the local mills as their occupation is listed as woollen spinners. Ted's youngest sister, Sarah, aged 12, is described as a nurse.

Despite being the home of several mills, Yeadon was at a high altitude and surrounded by green fields. It must have been a happy place compared to the crowded and dirty streets of Holbeck. However, a contemporary writer, Philemon Slater, described Yeadon in 1878 as 'noted for anything but its architecture' and said that it consisted of a 'bewildering labyrinth of yards and courts and intricate lanes'. This was certainly true of The Green, which despite its name was in the heart of the old part of the village and, according to Aireborough History Society, was known as Hell Square. There was a pub on The Green, officially the Oddfellows Arms but better known locally as the Rag and Louse.

However, there was another facility which was to prove hugely beneficial for the young Ted. The village had a highly successful cricket club which had already produced a number of players who went on to forge a career as club professionals. In 1867, when Ted Peate was only 12, the club hosted a match in which a United All England team played 22 men of Yeadon and District in a three-day game. Peate must surely have been in the crowd and if he was not already attached to the village club, he was soon to be. Yeadon's reputation as one of the most significant club sides in Yorkshire was further enhanced in 1877 when W.G. Grace appeared at the Yeadon ground in another challenge match, designed to boost both club and the professionals' coffers, when he brought his United South XI team to play a Yeadon 22. The story goes that W.G. was bowled for a duck and the elated bowler called John Tye was widely condemned for ruining the game as the crowd had come to see the famous Doctor Grace. It seems like another variant of the 'They've come to see me bat, not you bowl' anecdotes which abound about Grace. Peate appeared in this game, the first of many encounters with W.G., but featured with neither bat nor ball as the weather intervened with no play at all on the third and final day. Yeadon had reached 58/3, The South had scored 165 runs, 82 of them coming from Walter Gilbert, with Peate taking the catch which finally dismissed him. Incidentally, Gilbert's career was to end abruptly in disgrace in 1886 when he was sent to prison after pleading guilty to stealing money from his fellow players in a club match. He had gone into the changing room alone and was spotted rifling through their pockets and was caught red-handed with their cash. At the conclusion of his jail sentence, he was packed off to Canada by the family.

Peate was obsessive about cricket, as a tradesman in the town was to relate at a celebratory dinner held to mark Peate's trip to Australia in 1881. Yeadon club member Thomas Blatchley, who owned a chemist's shop in the village, said he had known Peate since he was a little boy. The *Wharfedale Observer* reported: 'He had a vivid recollection that Peate's first wicket was his (Mr Blatchley's) shop window. The window was then low down and three pickle bottles were exposed to view. He remembered Mr Ted took great delight in aiming at the middle one (laughter) and he had improved since then.'

Peate became a member of Yeadon in 1873 when he was 18 years of age and was quickly drafted into the first team. Mr Blatchley continued to tell his audience that coming home from his first appearance for his local club, Peate had told him that he had not done so well with the bat but had astonished himself with his success with the ball. Sadly, Yeadon's archives are lost and matches were not always covered in the local papers, which were always dependent upon the efficiency of the local club secretary to get them to the newspaper offices in time to meet a strict deadline.

After making his mark in the Yeadon team as a teenager, Peate opted in 1875 to join the Treloar Cricketing Clowns. The phenomenon of 'Clown Cricket' in the late 19th century was highly frowned upon by the cricketing authorities and was not treated seriously by the press – if they chose not to completely ignore it. Clown Cricket followed a basic premise: the organisers of the clown troupe would be paid a guaranteed sum to turn up and play a selected team of opponents drawn usually from a town, village or locality where a local fete or similar fundraising venture was being staged. The organisers of the event would hope to recoup the clown troupe's fees through gate money. The event itself was hardly serious and typically there would be a number of decent cricketers, such as Peate, in the clown side who would engage the locals in a 'match'. While the match was taking place, the clowns would be performing stunts on the outfield, mingling with the crowds and generally trying to create the entertainment to get the spectators laughing. If the 'real' cricketers were proving too good for the local lads and an early end was looming, then a couple of clowns might be called upon to bat or bowl with numerous falls, juggling, buckets of water, faux arguments and slapstick to liven things up. There were no set rules, the attraction being that there would be some decent cricket played in the midst of the mayhem.

Peate may have been persuaded to try clown cricket by two fellow member of the Yeadon club who had both joined the Casey Clown Cricketers but quickly renounced their allegiance. Both Matthew Myers and William Slater played alongside Peate for Yeadon and Myers went on to play for Yorkshire. Myers was eight years older than Peate and firmly established in the Yeadon side. He was a relative of the Myers family who employed Peate in their textile business, so it is feasible that he was able to interest Peate in earning funds in this way and advising him of the benefits and drawbacks of going down this route. Peate was only 20 years old and a summer of getting paid to travel the country, play a bit of cricket and enjoy a free meal in the evening would seem quite enticing, or at least much better than working long hours inside a hot woollen mill with its smells and heavy atmosphere.

So Peate signed some sort of contract with the most well-known of the clown cricket troupes run by Arthur Treloar to appear for them in 1876. Eric Midwinter, a doyen of the Association of Cricket Statisticians, dates the origins of clown cricket to the 1860s. *The Era*, a newspaper which ditched its political origins and became focused on theatrical and music hall adverts and reports, claims a rather improbable crowd of 75,000 at Alexandra Palace in April 1881 to see Drecona and Mousley's Comical Clown Cricketers. However, the two biggest names on the clown cricket circuit were Casey and Treloar. From Cornwall originally, Arthur Treloar actually had one first-class match under his belt, representing Middlesex against Oxford University in 1872. He also turned out that summer for Glamorgan against Radnorshire. However, he appears to have been a bit of a Victorian wide boy. He was also known as Thomas Treloar and his cricket experience took him far and wide as he had stints as a club professional in Yorkshire with Ilkley, Mirfield and Hunslet and there is a record of him also turning out as professional for East Hampshire CC. However, he was far more suited to money-making schemes than earning from his cricketing prowess. He saw the possibilities of clown cricket and put together a side, aggressively promoting the fundraising potential of combining some decent cricket with a few laughs for the less sport-minded.

In August 1875 the *Yorkshire Post* carried an advert which said 'the London Imperial Clown Cricketers are open to arrange one- or two-day matches in September. Terms on share or otherwise. Address Messrs Davis and Treloar, Northgate Hotel, Bradford.' The advert shows not only that the organisers were willing to negotiate a share of the gate or agree a fee but that there were two of them. They must have fallen out, for the following year Davis was advertising his troupe as 'the only London Imperial Clown Cricketers' and enquiries were directed to his Southampton address. Meanwhile, Treloar was advertising his rival band as the 'only legitimate and original London Imperial Clown Cricketers' and had taken out the following advert in *The Era*: 'Mr Treloar begs to inform his Friends, Cricketers and Patrons that he is in no way connected with any person using his name or title of his team (of which he captains) and that no engagements are genuine without his signature'. The rivalry was seemingly bitter. Davis took out an advert in *The Era* on 4 June 1876 seeking to fill vacant dates which ended 'also a vacancy for a good Knockabout Clown of repute. Will Carl Waller say why he did not keep his engagement?' That drew an immediate riposte in the following edition: 'Carl Waller, the Imperial Clown, begs to inform Mr Davis in answer to his advertisement that he refused his offer to engage him for his Clown Cricketers and cautions Mr Davis against using his name in any way which is likely to injure his reputation. Carl Waller never breaks engagements. Second season with Mr Treloar's Imperial Clown Cricketers.'

It was Davis' troupe which visited Peate's birthplace Holbeck, in the summer of 1876, provoking Casey to announce, in a *Yorkshire Post* advert of 28 June, their forthcoming match in neighbouring Hunslet in the following terms: 'Casey and Robson disclaim any connection with the troupe that played recently at Holbeck. We are neither London Imperial nor Royal and our title is simply as above.'

In this struggle between the rival impresarios Casey, Davis and Treloar, it was Treloar who came out on top. His engagements in the year Peate appeared typically started with a parade through the town or village where the event was to be staged with a burlesque singer called Ada Isaacs at the front. She was also the star turn after the event at an evening concert and refreshments where she performed, as the *Hastings Observer* put it, 'at great expense in a most magnificent dress'. It was not an easy life and in Whitsuntide week of 1876, Midwinter tracks Treloar's troupe as playing in Windsor on the Monday, heading to the Midlands for an engagement at Dudley Castle on the Tuesday and down to Hastings for the town's gala on the Wednesday.

In the autumn of 1876, Treloar raised his sights and took his clown cricketers on a tour of the United States. Peate declined to go. The *Boston Globe* of 12 September recorded that the Clown Cricketers and their captain, Arthur Treloar, would be appearing at the Boston Baseball Ground and his clowns would 'see that none of the spectators die of melancholy'. The *Globe* said there were 'five genuine cricketers' in the team but the match provoked little interest. Treloar then disappears from view. He seems to have ended his days across the Atlantic as Tom Melville's *History of Cricket in America* (1998) records him as being 'a peripatetic English sports promoter' who founded Omaha Cricket Club.

While clown cricket was a short-lived phenomenon which tided Peate over the summer of 1876, it was not a realistic long-term career move. The whole concept was frowned upon by the cricket establishment and the press. This disapproving article from the *Oxford Weekly News* of 2 August 1876 describes a match at Woodstock, Oxford, in which Peate probably played during his summer with Treloar's Cricketing Clowns which also went under the name of the Imperial Clown Cricketers. The match was part of a fete organised by the local branch of the Foresters, a mutual benefit society similar to the Oddfellows or Buffalos.

'This fete took place on Monday week and drew together about 2,000 persons. In a pecuniary sense it must have been a success to the Loyal Blenheim Lodge 5428. Treloar's Clown Cricketers with their "celebrated" band were engaged for the occasion and they were due at eleven but they did not arrive until two hours afterwards, which caused a good deal of waiting and inconvenience. The dinner then took place in the lodge room under the presidency of the mayor, Henry Lock Esq, to which a large number sat down. Subsequently the long-looked-for cricket match came off on the cricket ground of Blenheim Park, which resulted in a victory for the Clowns in the first innings, the second not being able to be played for lack of time. While the game was in progress, those of the clowns who were not otherwise engaged were set to amuse the onlookers of which there were a large number. Their jokes were those that in all probability our grandfathers may have condescended to smile at, being old, flat, stale and unprofitable and some of them very low indeed ... We are pleased to be able to state that the funds of the society will be augmented by some £60 by the fete in spite of all the drawbacks. Much sympathy is felt for the committee of the Lodge with respect to the failure of the "Imperials" as of course neither the society nor its officers are to be blamed, nevertheless it will doubtless be the first and last appearance of the "Imperial Clown Cricketers" in the precincts of Blenheim and Woodstock.'

The report drips with condescension and sneering while at the same time trying to avoid criticism of the local society worthies for staging the event in the first place and subjecting the good people of Blenheim and Woodstock to the 'very low' old jokes of the clowns.

The *Driffield Times* was equally scornful of clown cricket, its edition of 27 September 1879 describing the clowns who played a team of locals as 'amateur fools' who 'deserved to be held up for ridicule'. It was scathing about the entertainment, saying it was 'entirely wanting', with no artiste offering the slightest gymnastics or humour. The post-match merriment was equally dismal according to the paper: 'In the evening the troupe gave an entertainment in the Assembly Rooms; that is to say, it was announced as entertainment but it was as abortive an attempt as can possibly be conceived; there was not a voice among them, no notion of harmony, nothing whatever to recompense those who paid to hear them. Fortunately, there was only a small audience which grew smaller as the programme shortened.'

The name of this troupe was not given by the newspaper but there are hints that rather than being one of the well-established companies, it was in fact a rather ad hoc affair put together by some minor artistes.

The *West Sussex Journal* edition of 4 July 1876 did at least have a little praise for the cricketing prowess of Peate and his colleagues but it too was somewhat outraged that the match had even taken place at all. It does however suggest that the financial arrangement was somewhat different. The article indicates that Treloar paid Midhurst Cricket Club, based at Cowdray Park in Sussex, for hire of the ground and kept all the proceeds: 'Last Saturday Mr Treloar's Clown Cricketers paid us a visit and played against a team selected from the men employed on the building at Cowdray. Some few years ago the same party were engaged by our club to come down and play a two-day match. Then, from the novelty of the thing, the "clowns" must have netted a considerable amount of money as the ground was thronged with spectators; in fact it was so good that a second venture was determined upon by the enterprising Mr Treloar but this time the "exhibition" was a decided failure. After much fussing it is not surprising that the receipts at the gate were 30 shillings less than they were to have paid the club but under any circumstances they would never have got any spectators through a second time [i.e. for the second day of a two-day match]. Once was quite enough, either cricket or clowning, but the two together makes as unpalatable a mixture as can well be imagined. We pity the parties extremely for their bad taste in attempting to lower the standard of the noble game for there is no doubt about it, the clowns that were here on Saturday were really good cricketers, Mr Treloar himself being a first-class wicket keeper. We have not sent the score, for it is put in such an extraordinary form that it would take too long a time for us to decipher the names or runs. We must not forget to mention that the Midhurst Club is no better off for the clowns' visit, which is not surprising.'

The *Southern Daily News* of 14 August 1875 gives perhaps the longest description of a clown cricket match and deigns to give a scorecard of the event which was staged by Weymouth Cricket Club. The match was preceded by a march through the town by a band, with the cricketers on a horse-drawn wagon following and four performing clowns bringing up the rear. Following a lunch in a tent at the ground, the clown team, described as the London Imperial Clown Cricketers, batted first, with six of the team being proficient cricketers and five 'clowns being anything but adept at wielding the willow'. One of the Weymouth players was doing rather well and the newspaper says he was taken out of the attack to ensure the innings was not over too quickly. When Weymouth went in to bat the bowling was opened by Dick-a-Dick and King, 'the former a very fast, well-pitched bowler from Australia'. Scores were tied on a rain-affected second day when the game was closed, 'the Weymouth team having given the clowns such a thrashing as they have never experienced, there only being one wicket down in their second innings'. Still the engagement was not over as the clowns provided entertainment that evening at Weymouth's Royal Hotel which was so well attended that many were locked outside, unable to get in to see the show. One of the cricketers mentioned was Treloar, the man behind the most famous of the clown cricket companies.

This was the way in which Peate spent his summer of 1876. As a young man of 21 years, it was a way to see the world and earn decent money including board and lodgings with, as we have seen, dinners laid on in the evening. It was probably more lucrative than being a journeyman professional on the northern circuit, especially as his inexperience meant he did not have a great reputation that would have commanded a high fee in club cricket. Moreover, as a club professional his travelling expenses would have eaten into any fees earned. So the two clowning troupes, Treloar's group and Casey's Cricketers, were a not unrealistic proposition for a young man. Nor was it entirely a waste of his talent. During Peate's year with the side, Treloar's Clown Cricketers played a recorded 63 games although he would not have played in all. Weymouth may have given them a thrashing they had never experienced, but there were some good players in their ranks. Matthew Myers, who had played alongside Peate in the Yeadon side and was thus able to open his eyes into the pros and cons of clown cricket, used his experience to play for Yorkshire in 1876. He made 22 appearances over three seasons for the county, scoring 600 runs.

* * *

However, the clown cricketers were not a long-term proposition and in the 1880s the craze began to fade. Not everyone appreciated their antics and Peate himself records how Treloar's group had played a match in Sheffield, the bastion of Yorkshire cricket, where they were 'mobbed and sodded'. The scourge of clown cricket was even discussed at Lord's during an 1875 MCC committee meeting when a Dr Gaye complained that permission to stage a clown cricket match had been refused. The minutes record Dr Gaye stating that he 'received an answer which he thought was scarcely polite' but the secretary made the club's position clear: 'The Clown Cricketers were a burlesque upon cricket that could not be tolerated at Lord's Ground.'

While the 1870s and early 1880s were the heyday of clown cricket, it was to achieve new popularity in 1901 when Dan Leno, the leading performer on the Victorian music hall scene and who vies with Lily Langtry as the biggest showbusiness celebrity of the era, started 'Komik Kricket'. If Lord's had been remarkably sniffy about clown cricket, then the Surrey authorities must have seen the potential for some valuable income when they gave Leno permission for The Oval to be used to stage his 'Komik Kricket' team of 28 music hall stars against an Old England XIV captained by Tommy Dewar, the owner of the Scottish whisky company and the MP for Tower Hamlets. Dewar's team included several members of the Surrey ground staff including one current and one future Test player, William Lockwood and Ernie Hayes, plus wicketkeeper Fred Stedman, who that summer had set a Surrey record of 87 dismissals which was to stand until 1962.

The crowd was put at 18,000 and profits of more than £600 went to charity – in this case New Belgrave Hospital, the Licensed Victuallers Schools, the Cricketers' Fund and the Music Hall Benevolent Society. *The Sportsman* commented: 'If the shades of former players could have risen they would have been paralysed, for the ground on which they had made big scores was for the first time in its history given over to fun and frolic ... Never has Dan Leno, the greatest of our comics, had to work so hard.' Work hard he did, heading the parade to the venue dressed as a field marshal, batting in a khaki uniform with a top hat (the Boer War had ended just a few weeks beforehand), and fielding as a schoolgirl, then a pantomime camel and finally a 'savage chief'. The event was repeated in 1902 and 1903 with similar success but by 1904 Leno was in steep alcoholic decline, the event was abandoned and he died in October of that year. Clown cricket lingered on but the advent of World War One dealt its death blow.

Peate's attitude to clown cricket is not clear. Many years later he gave a rare interview to the doyen of Yorkshire cricket Alfred Pullin, who wrote under the pen name of

Old Ebor in the *Yorkshire Evening Post,* in which he discussed his experience without any sense of shame or regret. He did reveal that he approached Treloar rather than the other way round, and confirms that he took soundings from fellow cricketers who had already been on the clown circuit. He said: 'Some eight or nine professionals had been engaged by Casey and Robson as clown cricketers so I suppose I was fired with the same ambition and joined the rival troupe. We finished our tour at Sheffield by getting well mobbed and sodded. The "grinders" saw no fun in booby cricket; they preferred the genuine article and gave us an emphatic reminder of the fact. The company consisted of eight acrobats, eight talking clowns and eight cricketers. Of course, I could do a bit of talking when I thought it necessary and I made one attempt to figure as an acrobat. It was at Newport Pagnell. One of our professional acrobats was exhibiting his dexterity in hanging downwards by the toes. I thought I would show how easy it was and attempted the same feat. Somehow the toes wouldn't stick and I fell to the ground on my head. I at once came to the conclusion that I was not a born acrobat.'

Peate clearly had talent at this age but it was obvious that if he had any ambition to play first-class cricket then clown cricket was not going to enhance his prospects. After another winter working in the mill, Peate signed up to play as a professional with Carlisle for 1877. The Settle to Carlisle railway line had been opened the previous year and so it was possible to catch a direct train from Leeds and up through the scenic line, although it would have involved considerable travelling time. Unfortunately, all Carlisle's records were lost in a flood and the local newspapers (relying on submissions sent in by the individual clubs) carried scant reports. The *Carlisle Patriot* notes his first game for them was on 21 May at home to Kendal and the decent crowd would have been satisfied with his five-wicket haul. Three days later he took six wickets, five of them clean bowled, against the West of Scotland. Alas the full bowling figures are not given and the reports confine themselves to strict reportage of the action with no commentary. He was not always to the fore. On 15 June Carlisle scored 147 against Dumfries and then bowled out their opponents for just 22 but Peate went wicketless, although he did take a catch. It was while engaged at Carlisle that Peate also played for the club against the United South side mentioned on page 13 – his second contest against W.G. Grace.

However, we do know that Peate was at this time a fast bowler and we do have a flavour of his prowess from the Lancashire and England batsman Allan Steele. Just as Peate is the first name on the honours board at Lord's for bowling, so Steel is the first on the board for Test centuries at the ground. In 1888 he and the Hon. Robert Henry Lyttelton (who played no county cricket but was a regular for sides such as the Gentlemen of England) penned a book about cricket which formed part of the *Badminton Library of Sports and Pastimes*. It must have been Steele who had experience of Peate playing for Carlisle which led him to write: 'We have had some excellent left-handed bowlers in England, and there can be no doubt that every team should possess one of this sort if possible. Peate for some years enjoyed the reputation of being the best left-hander in England, and rightly so ... When Peate first began to play cricket, he was a very fast, high-actioned bowler, and the writer remembers thirteen or fourteen years ago finding him on the slow sticky wicket of the Carlisle ground very nasty to play. He subsequently altered his pace to slow, and it is a remarkable fact that, though a fast bowler once, and still a young man, he has now lost the power of sending down a really fast ball.'

Peate described his season with Carlisle as 'fairly successful' in his interview with Pullin given a decade after his first-class career was over. However, his contract was not renewed; the travelling was probably proving arduous for Peate, while Carlisle may have decided to look elsewhere. At this time a Yeadon resident called Amos Marshall, a slow bowler who made one appearance for Yorkshire, was professional with his home town club and had provided coaching to the young Peate. It was Marshall who recommended Peate to Manningham, an ambitious club on the northern periphery of Bradford. They were expecting a fast bowler. Instead they found that the 23-year-old who turned up at their ground for the 1878 season had spent the winter developing his spin technique.

Peate explained in his interview with Pullin: 'Before going to Manningham I was engaged as a warp twister with Messrs Myers and Co at Yeadon and having time during the working hours of the winter to practise, I made the most of it. I used to bowl in a weaving shed with the bales of Red Dicks around. Red Dicks, I should explain, were bales of mungo [higher quality cloth recycled from rags] intended for the making of red shawls for the China market. I made a copy of Amos Marshall's style. The result was that I found I could keep a good length and get some twist on the ball and in the spring I had put the winter's practice to such good use that I came out as a slow bowler. My first match with Manningham was against Yeadon. As I had been engaged as a fast bowler, the Manningham club were rather surprised to find on taking up my engagement with them that I was bowling slow. In the match with Yeadon, however, I bowled fast and took seven wickets for 28 runs. That was the last time I bowled fast. I knew that my slow bowling, with an occasional fast delivery, was my forte and I stuck to it.'

Before he had played his first game for Manningham, Ted's mother died at the age of 50 on 6 April. He oversaw her burial in the graveyard of her home town, Yeadon. Peate had no time to mourn – he had a living to earn in Bradford. For Manningham Peate was a regular wicket-taker and it was while playing for them that he had his first recorded encounter with a man who was to have a big influence on his career – Tom Emmett. Already established as a key member of the Yorkshire squad, Emmett was renowned for his good humour and Peate found a soulmate. Emmett always took a light-hearted view of cricket but was a deadly fast bowler and a punishing left-handed batsman. Stories of his joking are legion. For example, after a bad day in the field with a host of dropped catches he supposedly told his team 'there's an epidemic here today and it ain't catching'. He was renowned for bowling wides and Lord Hawke was to describe him as 'the greatest character that ever stepped on a cricket field, a merry wag who could never lose heart or temper' and another cricketing lord, Harris of Kent, said of him, 'I have never known a keener or merrier cricketer than dear old Tom. He was as hard as a board and active as a cat.' Emmett's sunny disposition earned him plenty of leeway from Hawke and despite his preference to have a good time rather than win at all costs, he managed to survive at Yorkshire until 1888 when he was 47 years old and had 9,000 first-class runs and 1,500 wickets to his name.

Emmett had joined Yorkshire from a professional role at Keighley – demanding £5 per game for his services – and, with Yorkshire not playing, he was making a return appearance for them when Manningham were the visitors on 22 June 1878. It was a comfortable win for Keighley but the scorebook shows that Emmett was bowled by Peate for nine runs. Doubtless he took note and, who knows, found out more about the clown cricketer over a post-match pint. This match was followed on 20 July by a rather strange one as Manningham took on their great local rivals Windhill and Peate took nine wickets as Windhill were all out for

29. Chasing a seemingly easy target, Manningham were dismissed for only 25.

That summer, Peate was invited back to his nursery club for his first of many encounters with Australia. The three-day match, which started on 20 August, was the centrepiece of the Yeadon Feast and Peate was included in a Yeadon and District 18 to take on the tourists. The Australian captain Dave Gregory was rested and replaced by a student at Stoneyhurst College called Tobin, who just happened to be born in Australia, while star batsman Charles Bannerman was also missing, reported in the *Yorkshire Post* to be 'prostrated by hard work'. The locals were all out for 91 but hit back by dismissing the Australians for 54 with Peate doing most of the damage with 5-24. The match ended in a draw – Yeadon scored 71 in their second innings while Peate was wicketless as the Australians reached 55/4 when time ran out.

At the end of the summer, Manningham travelled to Scarborough to play in the town's seaside festival of cricket. Although his team were well beaten by an innings, Peate's performance caught the eye of one cricket-mad vicar with connections in high places. He was the Rev. Edmund Carter, and he invited Peate to play alongside him in the Yorkshire Gentlemen's team which was playing Scarborough in the festival's next game. It was to be a turning point in Peate's life.

Chapter 2

The Professional

IT WAS while playing for Manningham that Peate caught the eye of the county selectors. He was later to put on record his gratitude to Rev. Edmund Carter for providing the opportunity to put his talents in the shop window. Carter was the vicar of St Martin cum Gregory in York and the driving force behind the Yorkshire Gentlemen Cricket Club, whose ground now forms the car park of York District Hospital. Another to credit the clergyman with opening the door to a Yorkshire career was Lord Hawke, although the two were spotted in very different circumstances – the well-bred Hawke with his appearances for the Yorkshire Gentlemen, the mill worker Peate toiling for working-class Manningham against Scarborough. Carter was a cricket fanatic and devotee of the Scarborough club (his family were from nearby Slingsby) and it may not be an over-exaggeration to state that he put his cricketing interests at least on a par with his clerical duties.

Rev. Carter was one of those who gave an interview to cricket writer Alfred Pullin and he expanded upon the lucky break which led to Peate's discovery: 'The circumstances under which Peate came out are certainly interesting. We found we were a man short for Yorkshire Gentlemen v

Scarborough at the close of the carnival of 1878. In the pavilion I asked if there was anyone at liberty who would like to play. A young fellow said he was at liberty. "Could he bowl?" "Yes, he could bowl a little bit." So I told him to change and come out. I was keeping wicket and I put him on to bowl first. I never had occasion to take him off. He had a marvellously easy action and a good length with a break from leg. I asked him where he had played. "With Manningham" was the reply. I told him he must send me his records as he would have to play for Yorkshire. And this was how Ted Peate was introduced into the Yorkshire team.' The match in question started on 16 September and Peate was in top form for the Gentlemen's team which appears in some reports under the name of its captain, F. Wheeler. The Gentlemen scored 133 and when Scarborough replied with 158, Peate took six wickets. Chasing 68 to win, time ran out when Scarborough were 53/4. Peate had taken another three wickets.

As a Yorkshire committeeman, Carter remembered Peate from that performance in the late summer of 1878 and arranged for him to play in a trial match for players who might be considered good enough to represent the county at Bramall Lane, Sheffield, in June 1879. Although termed colts, Peate was now 24 years old and had been making a name for himself at Manningham. The two sides – both of 13 players – were named after the two captains, Rochford and Horner, with Peate playing for the latter. He took ten of the 12 wickets to fall as Rochford's team were all out for 70. Not surprisingly, the *Yorkshire Post* said his bowling was way above his peers and he was certain to make a mark in the future. His 19 not out in the Horner first innings, which amassed just 83, must also have caught the eye. The *Yorkshire Post* was to persist in believing that Peate could make a good batsman for the remainder of his county career even if the statistics suggest differently. The following day the Rochford XIII were rapidly dismissed, scoring just 56. Peate's share was 7-26. In an interview shortly before his death, Peate said that a Yorkshire committeeman had come up to him and said 'Ah Peate, I saw you were not trying in the second innings. You only wanted to encourage them.' Even so Peate had made a big impression and the *Post*'s correspondent remarked 'the colts, with few exceptions, are a fine, smart lot and much above the average standard. Peate is unquestionably a good bowler and a hard, punishing, if not a very finished batter.' With such spectacular figures and attention from the colts match, it was inevitable that the Yorkshire captain (at this point Tom Emmett) would take notice and Peate duly made his Yorkshire debut just two days later at Nottingham. None of the 25 other players involved in the colts game were called up, although nine others were to appear at least once for the county later: Irwin Grimshaw 125 appearances; Fred Lee 105; John Rawlin 27; Henry Lockwood 16; Henry Taylor 3; Walter Aspinall 2; Henry Mosley 2; Henry Robinson 1; George Lee 1.

The Yorkshire team which Peate forced his way into in 1879 was less than 20 years old and its modus operandi somewhat opaque. It is widely accepted that Yorkshire County Cricket Club was born in March 1861 at the Adelphi Hotel in Sheffield (the site is now occupied by the Crucible Theatre, home to the World Snooker Championship). At this meeting the Sheffield Public Match Committee resolved 'that immediate steps be taken to raising a public match fund to defray the expenses of playing county and public matches that may be played on the Bramall Lane ground in Sheffield and that the offices of the various clubs of the town be requested to lend their cordial assistance towards raising such funds and forming a committee for carrying out the same'. Professional players at various clubs were contacted to find out their terms for representing a team which would face Surrey and call itself Yorkshire. By 1863 the following resolution was passed: 'that a county club be formed, the annual subscription to be not less than 10/6d (52.5p) per member'. A proper county club had been formed, with its rules and officers in place.

Even so, there was opposition to the appropriation of the Yorkshire name from other major towns and cities of the county, not least Bradford. The Bradford Football Club (which played the rugby football code, not association football) was already considered the strongest – and richest – in the north. A measure of its strength was that the Barbarians rugby club was formed not in London but at a hotel in Bradford after a team of well-connected southern players headed north to play the famous Bradford club as a regular fixture. However, its cricketing arm was less influential. Sheffield was better organised and better motivated and thus emerged as the cricketing power in the county. This Sheffield-based Yorkshire club made its first appearance at The Oval on 4 June 1863. However, it would be unfair to accuse it of Sheffield bias. Three players were from Sheffield, the same number from Huddersfield.

The aim was to stage top quality cricket and also earn enough money to pay the best players who would attract the biggest crowds. So right from the start, professional cricketers dominated the side. It was not that amateurs were necessarily inferior players, it was just that they had business or other interests which would prevent them playing (sometimes giving word at short notice). A professional, on the other hand, was eager to earn as much money as possible. The life of a professional was not the gateway to riches. One of those who played in The Oval match, John Thewlis, who was the first to score a century for the county, ended his days heaving laundry for a living. It was for this reason that in

1870 Edwin (Ned) Stephenson was awarded the first benefit match at which gate receipts were handed directly to the player as a token of appreciation for his services. Similar benefits occurred at regular intervals but Peate was never to be a recipient, being dispensed with before completing ten years at the club. However, some players were awarded benefits long after they had retired if they had fallen on hard times. Another member of that Oval match, George Anderson, played his last game for Yorkshire in 1869 but in 1895 was granted a benefit which earned him £300. Luke Greenwood – also picked for that 1863 match and an umpire at the famous 1882 Oval 'Ashes' Test – fell on hard times and was given a ten shilling a week pension in the 1890s. In 1883, with Peate the star bowler in the Yorkshire team and indeed the country, he would have noted how his colleague Ephraim Lockwood made £591 from his benefit match. He must have looked forward to a substantial windfall heading his way when his ten years were up.

The 1881 census listed 211 men in England who gave their occupation as a cricketer. One of them was 83 years old, so retired professional cricketer is a more accurate description, while one, Peter Rogers, of Cowley in Oxfordshire, was just 14. Given that there were ten active county teams at the time and many of them, but not Yorkshire, were inclined to favour places for amateur gentlemen, it is clear that there was a large body of men who considered that their living was heavily, if not exclusively, reliant upon playing at club level or coaching at a public school (which suggests a high level of skill). Peate was emerging from this class of men, earning a fee from his club appearances during the summer and topping it up with work in the mills over the winter. The amount a club professional might earn varied and was a balance between the ambitions of the club and the negotiating skills of the player but it was more lucrative than what might be earned in almost all manual jobs. Tom Emmett, who was to have a long career with Yorkshire, was earning between two shillings and sixpence (12.5p) and five shillings (25p) per game in club cricket with Keighley but demanded £5 per game when Yorkshire came calling. They paid. One thing, though, was common to both club and county players. It was a precarious job, as an injury or loss of form would have meant disaster. In 1886 the *Athletic News* cricket supplement and club directory listed 112 clubs in the West Riding of Yorkshire with 55 professionals engaged by 49 clubs. County games were rarely held on a Saturday and so the county professionals might also be approached by a club on an ad hoc basis to pick up a little extra cash. There were no leagues at this point so the notion of hiring a Yorkshire county player for a one-off match was more to boost the gate receipts than to ensure a crucial victory – although the factor of local pride and putting one over your fiercest rivals should not be underestimated.

It was common for the professionals to drink during the game. After all, many of the crowd were doing the same and it was widely accepted that the players would be 'treated', i.e. bought a drink. The authorities frowned upon this but found it impossible to stamp out. Indeed, any attempt to stop spectators buying a drink for the professional was resented by buyer and recipient alike. Professor Wray Vamplew in a treatise on *Alcohol and the Sportsperson*, wrote: 'At the end of the 19th century cricketers still turned to alcohol during a day's play and were advised that on a hot day "beer and stout are too heady and heavy" and "ginger beers are too sticky" and that "shandy and claret and soda are the most thirst quenching and cleanest to the palate".' It wasn't just Yorkshire – in his splendid *The Autobiography of Edward Pooley*, Rodney Ulyate quotes from interviews given by the controversial England wicketkeeper: 'There was more comradeship among the pros of my time than there is today. We were a hail-fellow-well-met, jolly lot of chaps … In the evening when the cricket was over we used to be allowed to have a smoke and drink outside the pavilion and thus the leading members of the clubs became acquainted with each other and there was much conviviality and good feeling.'

But the conviviality could get out of hand. In 1881 the *Yorkshire Post* published a letter from a reader in Bradford writing under the pseudonym of 'Old Cricketer'. The contents sound suspiciously as though the author was someone who was close to the team. While in itself the letter is not proof of bad behaviour, it does confirm that there were those who were unhappy at the conduct of the professionals. One reason for their poor performances was said to be treating. The letter writer said: 'It may appear at first sight to be ungenerous to object to a good batsman or a good bowler having a glass of beer. But when we consider how glass after glass deteriorates the men and makes them unfit to either bat, bowl or field well, he is their best friend who abstains from putting them in the way of temptation. I know of one of the very best bats in Yorkshire utterly ruined by the wretched system of treating. After making 40 and 40 not out against the best club in the county he was not sober for a week, being continually treated by fools that had more brass than brains.'

However, times were changing when Peate broke into the county scene. The concept of what Rob Light in his work on the *Victorian Cricketer Reconsidered* describes as the 'respectable cricketer' was emerging and codes of conduct and behaviour were being established. Before 1880 the professional was 'a rumbustious individual off the field, prone to disputes with his fellow professionals and cricket administrators'. However, and particularly on the county circuit, the respectable cricketer concept increasingly frowned upon poor behaviour and the codes of conduct brought 'a new level of recognition and status. This served to endorse the strict moral guidance, social deference and economic constraints that the regulations imposed upon the players.' The idea that cricket was not just a game to be won but one with standards to uphold was emerging even among professionals (although, as we shall see, adherence to this code was somewhat flexible).

This was all well and good for sides where amateur players abounded and could impose their authority more easily by simply not selecting (and thus not paying) a professional who did not toe the line. An exclusively professional team like Yorkshire found it more difficult to mend their ways. The new professional like Peate upon entering the Yorkshire fold found a drinking culture and the Victorian equivalent of a playboy mentality. Anyone who tried to impose higher standards was liable to be scoffed at. So, from the moment Peate first came into the Yorkshire team in 1880, the tide was changing, The professional cricketer was expected to be, as Light put it, 'more sophisticated and more temperate in his behaviour – or more precisely in the way he conformed to the predilections of middle-class morality'. Yorkshire were just a little behind the flow but the new attitude was to be firmly emphasised by the arrival of the powerful character of Lord Hawke as captain and driving force behind the county team. He recognised Yorkshire were a good team with some great players but not a great team.

Peate's selection for Yorkshire brought an immediate improvement in his financial fortune. The pay was good and the kudos which came from being a county star was irreplaceable. The drawback was that it was a short and precarious life. David Frith's book *By His Own Hand* details the many cricketers whose life spiralled after the financial and psychological pressures brought on by the termination of a first-class cricket career. Surrey's Billy Brockwell, ten years younger than Peate, who played seven times for England and on more than 300 occasions for Surrey, was reduced to living in a roofless hovel when he was pointed out to Lord Hawke, who was playing golf at Sundridge Golf Club with Sir Home Gordon. In his autobiography, Gordon states: 'We took steps in some measure to remedy what was the saddest instance that ever came to my knowledge,' though what those steps were is not explained. Brockwell is just one example of many who fell on hard times. One thing which separates Brockwell from Peate is that he was given a testimonial when his career ended. Peate was not.

At the time Peate was playing first-class cricket, it was a summer-only existence with no provision for earning over the winter. The magazine *London Life* wrote in 1863, 'a short and merry [career] is all the professional can hope as regards his cricketing existence – younger and more brilliant men tread upon his heels. Popular applause is proverbially capricious and the smoking, drinking and good living during the summer contrasted with the greens and bacon all through the winter … few of the professionals have a shilling left when the winter had drained their store.' Even so, it was better pay in far more convivial conditions than the mills, mines and factories of the working man from which most professionals sprang. Plus there was the chance for a little extra income from coaching, appearances and selling equipment to perhaps set oneself up in business – a shop perhaps or a pub – although this may have proven hazardous to the Yorkshire 'ale cans'.

We do not know how much Peate earned but the *Athletic News* in 1895 (when Peate's first-class career was over) stated that most first-class counties paid a professional £5 for each home match and £6 for an away match. However, the professional had to pay for his own travel and accommodation. The best indication of Peate's earnings can be gleaned from Keith Sandford's paper on Victorian professionals. He states that a good quality professional earned an average of £100 a year in 1875 which rose to an average of £250 a year in 1900. At the same time the income of a labourer rose from an average of £80 in 1875 to £100 in 1900. Sandford also pays tribute to Lord Hawke's efforts in improving the lot of the professional: 'Ironically it was aristocratic amateur Lord Hawke who most clearly identified the major reasons why professional cricketers relapsed into poverty and who tried hardest to save them from the normal pitfalls ... He did his best, albeit in an autocratic manner, to improve the image of the Yorkshire professional cricketers by teaching them to have pride in themselves. He insisted on proper discipline, decent and tidy dress, punctuality and respectable demeanour at all times.'

George Pinder, the wicketkeeper whose county career ended the year after Peate's started, spoke of his earnings in a letter: 'We only got £5 per match wherever we went and the largest number of matches I played in one season was 24. That was £120. Out of that I had to pay my hotel bills, my railway travelling and maintain my home, wife and four children. We started in May and gave up in September and then seven months to get over.' It was a theme taken up by Edward Pooley, who said: 'Like other cricketers of my time, I got little "fat" out of some of our excursions ... [William] Mortlock and I were playing at Edinburgh with the old United [South of England] Eleven and when we got back to the Elephant and Castle found we had no more than 1s 4d [6p] in our pockets between us.'

Good performances might earn 'talent money' – a bonus approved by the committee or even a donation from the spectators ('passing round the hat'). An example of this occurred in a charity match Peate played in on 8 July 1879 sandwiched between Yorkshire's games against Nottinghamshire and Lancashire. To raise funds for Bradford Infirmary top players from the Airedale District were pitched against the Bradford District in a 12-a-side match. Peate, representing the Bradford District courtesy of his allegiance to Manningham, took 9-34 and 6-37 but he was reckoned to be outshone by an Airedale player, P. Watmough from Saltaire, who took 8-24 and 3-3 when time was called on the Bradford District's second innings. Crucially, Watmough also scored 38 and 12 with the bat and the *Bradford Observer* recorded, 'he was presented with £1 12 shillings contributed by the spectators in admiration of the excellent cricket he had shown'. This appears to be a match between professionals attached to local clubs as the *Observer* reported that 'most' players gave their services for free and so there were minimal expenses resulting in around £40 for the infirmary.

Sandford also reveals that MCC fee for playing for the Players against the Gentlemen was £10 and this was subsequently viewed as the going rate for playing a representative match. Of course, a high status cricketer such as W.G. Grace (who technically was an amateur but demanded large sums in expenses for his services) would earn more but it was a risky business for a professional like Peate to demand a couple of pounds more for a game – there was always someone emerging from the club scene to challenge his pre-eminence. Indeed, having held off the challenge of Billy Bates, it was the emergence of Bobby Peel which helped end Peate's Yorkshire career.

The dangers of demanding more money were starkly illustrated by a 'strike' of professionals William Gunn of Nottinghamshire, and Surrey quartet George Lohmann, Tom Richardson, Bobby Abel and Tom Hayward before the Ashes match at The Oval in 1896. They wrote to the Surrey committee asking for the match fee to be increased from £10 to £20. The five pointed out that the Australians were receiving £1,700 for the fixture and the Surrey club would make a similar amount. Their unhappiness was heightened by the fact that the amateurs in the England team would be getting far more than them in 'expenses' – W.G. Grace was widely known to insist on £50 to play. The Surrey men would also have known about the unusual circumstances of their team-mate Walter Read, an England captain, who received a salary of £150 but did not appear to do any work in his role as 'assistant secretary' to the club. He was also the recipient of a railway season ticket plus expenses of four guineas (£4 4 shillings) per game and a bonus of £100 after making an agreed number of appearances for his county. The editor of *Wisden* showed little sympathy for the strikers and wrote: 'The earnings of the players have certainly not risen in proportion to the immensely increased popularity of cricket during the last 20 years but to represent the average professional as an ill-treated or downtrodden individual is, I think, a gross exaggeration.' Surrey refused to countenance the players' conditions and Richardson, Abel and Hayward wrote suitably contrite apologies and were re-instated in the team. Lohmann and Gunn held out and Surrey sent an urgent message to Yorkshire, from where Bobby Peel and George Hirst hot-footed it down to London to take part in the English victory. A hard-nosed Yorkshireman would not pass up the opportunity of £10!

A top professional would also rely heavily on his benefit. Alas, Peate did not get one. George Ulyett, his colleague for Yorkshire and England, did and made more than £1,000. However, Peate was disposed of before he had the required ten years of service and the Yorkshire committee did not want to set a precedent by waiving the rule. The main source of income from a benefit was the money taken from the turnstiles going to the player. It could be lucrative but if the match selected for the benefit was ruined by rain, then the player missed out.

The brilliant England and Sussex batsman K.S. Ranjitsinhji had a somewhat blasé view about professionals. For a man who would become Maharajah (effectively ruler) of the Indian princely state of Nawanagar he probably did not have the greatest insight into the life of a professional who had risen from working-class poverty in England. In his 1897 *The Jubilee Book of Cricket* his chapter on professionals somewhat smugly declared: 'The demand for players who have been first-class to fill posts at clubs and schools is far in excess of the supply. A first-class cricketer, whose character is good, can rely with certainty upon obtaining on his retirement from county cricket a suitable and well-paid berth, which he will be capable of filling for many years. Frequently, too, their fame and popularity help cricketers to find good businesses upon their retirement, when usually they have a certain amount of money, gained from their benefit match, to invest.'

In the late 1870s, as Peate was beginning to emerge, Yorkshire's results were disappointing despite having some of the leading players in the country – Tom Emmett and Allen Hill were the best fast bowlers, George Pinder the best wicketkeeper, Ephraim Lockwood second only to W.G. Grace as a batsman, George Ulyett and Louis Hall exciting new finds. Yet in 1877 Yorkshire were deemed eighth of nine counties in the 'championship', the rankings drawn up by the MCC committee. Once again the behaviour of the Yorkshire players was considered a chief factor in their disappointing results. With that typical language of the time which said much but hid more, Rev. R.S. Holmes, the first Yorkshire cricket historian said, 'It may have been a fact that some of the playing members were lacking in that self-control which is indispensable to conspicuous success.' A more recent historian might have been less careful in his choice of words. Derek Hodgson, in his *Official History of Yorkshire County Cricket Club*, described them as 'a bunch of ale cans', a fine

Yorkshire expression. This was the milieu which Peate was to enter.

* * *

The summer of 1879 was one of the wettest on record and most games were curtailed badly by the weather. So bad were conditions that it was the last time that no first-class player scored 1,000 runs in the summer. Peate's debut match against Nottinghamshire was no exception with standing water on the outfield. Put into bat, the Yorkshire innings was a disaster as they were skittled out for just 49, Peate making a duck as he was out lbw. The home side made 176 and Peate took 2-39. Yorkshire were two without loss when the rain came down and the match abandoned.

Peate had done enough to earn a second chance. A day later he was due to play Surrey at Hull in again terribly wet conditions. Surrey were put into bat and skittled out for 50 but Peate played little part. Tom Emmett preferred to use the fearsome roundarm bowler Allen Hill. It was a good decision as Hill recorded his best career figures of 7-14 and Billy Bates, who was to feature throughout Peate's first-class career, took the other three wickets. The new boy Peate was given just four overs. When Yorkshire batted they made 118 but Peate was again out for a duck. In the second innings Peate wasn't handed the ball at all. This time Bates did the main damage with six wickets with Emmett taking the other four as the visitors were all out for 58, giving Yorkshire victory by an innings and ten runs.

However, Peate did not have to wait long to make a big impression. His chance came along a couple of days after the Surrey thrashing at Bramall Lane, scene of his triumph in the trial match, with Kent the visitors. Batting first the Yorkshire side made 114, Peate contributing one, which was his first run for Yorkshire, before he was handed the ball to open the bowling to Lord Harris, the Kent captain. Peate's accuracy and skills made the Kent scoring 'tediously slow' according to the newspaper correspondents and when they were all out for 97, he had sent down 42 overs and taken 6-39. The *Yorkshire Post* was impressed enough to write, 'Peate fairly established his reputation as a bowler.' In the second Kent innings he returned virtually identical figures of 6-38 as Yorkshire ran out winners by 61 runs, the verdict this time being 'Peate's bowling was again very effective.' The following day the paper could run a more considered verdict rather than a deliver a precis of the action. Its *'Cricket Notes'* column opined: 'The colt Peate made a great mark and has suddenly bowled himself into a county player for the present. He fields his own bowling well, has an excellent pitch and is always on the sticks. This makes the third left-handed bowler in the eleven.'

A county player or not, Peate was in action the day after his Kent exploits, turning out for his home club Yeadon against Pittsmoor (Sheffield). Skill-wise, he was way above the ordinary club bowler and Pittsmoor were skittled out for 38 and 55, Peate taking 11 wickets as his side coasted to an innings and six runs victory. That kept him firmly in the eyes of the Yorkshire captain, Tom Emmett, who picked him for the return match against Nottinghamshire, once again at Bramall Lane. Emmett, a fine fast bowler himself who had played for England but was possibly seen as beginning to lose his pace, may have had regrets as Peate went wicketless as Notts made 117. However, Peate's skills came into their own as the visitors batted a second time. He took 5-38, sending down 30 of the 62 overs needed to polish off Notts and complete a straightforward victory. The *Yorkshire Post* continued its praise of the new find: 'It was a feather in the colt's cap to clean bowl the two Nottinghamshire cracks, Daft and Oscroft.' The correspondent was referring to

Richard Daft, whose first-class career spanned 33 years and included almost 10,000 runs (in the 14 seasons from 1864 he topped the Notts run list for 11 of them) and William Oscroft, another prolific run compiler who was in the W.G. Grace team to tour Australia in 1873/74.

After the high of beating their great rivals Nottinghamshire, the Yorkshire players again failed to carry their form through. They were beaten in quick succession by Lancashire (by an innings), Derbyshire and Kent. The novice Peate was less effective, although still ended up with a 'five-for' in the Kent match. This was a mere appetiser for Yorkshire's biggest match of the season – against Gloucestershire, who had been recognised as county champions in 1873, 1874, 1876 and 1877 (without a formal County Championship and fixture programme, the champion county was the one recognised by the press based on matches won). It was not just their status which made this the biggest game of the season, it was the presence of W.G. Grace in the ranks of the visitors which drew a huge crowd to Sheffield. Grace, who celebrated his 31st birthday just days before the fixture, was already a legendary figure in the game but he missed much of the 1879 season because he was doing the final practical part of his medical examination. He was to qualify in November of that year and it was the first season in ten years that he did not complete 1,000 first-class runs (although, previously noted, nor did anyone else in that wet, dreary summer).

The *Yorkshire Evening Post* report on 29 July 1879 stated: 'Of all the county fixtures, no match in the Yorkshire programme has ever attracted the monster attendance at Bramall Lane as the one under notice'. How would Yorkshire's new but inexperienced spin maestro fare against the batting superstar who was about to earn his nickname 'The Doctor' and who opened the batting for Gloucestershire? The

Evening Post's verdict was: 'Peate's bowling was noteworthy. From his first 20 overs only eight singles were made. A tremendous roar proclaimed the downfall of the crack who played one of Peate's [deliveries] into his wicket. We never saw him hit so tamely and he was evidently not at home with Peate. He was in for one hour and five minutes for his 13.' The modern cricket follower may reflect ruefully on the over rate: Yorkshire sent down 168 overs on that first day with Peate doing the bulk of work with 60 of them, although these were the days of an over consisting of four balls so it is the modern equivalent of 112 overs. He took 5-71 as Gloucestershire were bowled out for 253. There was still time for Yorkshire to reach 30/2 before stumps on day one.

Yorkshire wickets tumbled on the second day and they were all out 125 runs behind. They followed on and scored 195, leaving Gloucestershire a target of 71 to win. It was time for Peate to really establish himself as not just a prospect, but already a glittering talent. Batting line-ups were a lot more fluid in this era and Grace declined to open the batting, sending in his brother, E.M. Grace, as he no doubt prepared to settle back and watch Gloucester cruise home. Instead Peate and his right arm off-breaking partner Billy Bates quickly reduced the visitors to 39/5 and W.G. was forced to don his pads. To no avail – he was bowled by Bates for a duck and, despite some resistance from the third Grace brother in the Gloucester team, Fred, the innings closed with Yorkshire still seven runs in front. Bates shared great similarities with Peate. A better batsman than Peate (he scored 10,000 first-class runs) he took 299 wickets, 15 of them in Tests, and died when a cold became pneumonia. Born a few weeks after Peate, he died just a few weeks before Peate suffered the same fate. Pneumonia was also responsible for the demise of Fred Grace who, barely a year after this defeat at the hands of Yorkshire, was to die from the infection.

The *Evening Post* described the match as one of the most exciting county matches ever played and went on to reveal that the committee presented George Ulyett (who scored 98 in the Yorkshire second innings) with £5 while Peate and Bates were both handed £2. It might seem somewhat unfair that Ulyett's 98 runs was considered more valuable than Peate's 11 wickets but he was the more established player, being in his sixth season with the county and a Test player. Not only that, he seems to have been a very popular figure in the Yorkshire dressing room and was widely known by his nickname Happy Jack. In contrast Peate was very much the young novice and would probably have been very happy with the £2 bonus which was almost twice as much as he earned in a week in his mill working days.

Yorkshire captain Tom Emmett highlighted this match when he was interviewed by Old Ebor (alias Alfred Pullin) for the book *Talks With Old Cricketers* to reflect on his career. Emmett related that at lunch, Gloucestershire were 34/2, requiring just 27 more with eight wickets remaining, W.G. among them. Emmett admitted that his side looked doomed: '"What odds will you lay Tom?" asked Bates. "Fifty to one," was my rash reply. Bates handed me a shilling and took the odds. An hour and a half afterwards I had to pay'. Such action, which might bring severe disciplinary action today, could have backfired as Emmett took the catch which dismissed Fred Grace. 'Had the catch been missed and the fact that I had laid a bet of 50 to one against Yorkshire been known, the committee or others would certainly have made remarks,' confessed Emmett.

It was not all plain sailing for Peate. Within a week of the Gloucestershire high, Yorkshire were beaten by an innings at Derby. Their opponents won only two matches that season (although Derbyshire had only six matches on their fixture list) – both against Yorkshire, which possibly highlights the soft centre at the heart of Emmett's team. It was a humbling defeat. Peate failed to take a wicket and proved again he was no great shakes with the bat as he failed to score above five in this period. Despite the blank at Derby, Emmett continued to show his faith in Peate in the next match which was at Huddersfield against Middlesex. The visitors were moving smoothly as they reached 82/2 before Emmett finally threw the ball to Peate. There was instant success as the Honourable Alfred Lyttleton (who was capped for England at both cricket and football and would later be a Cabinet member in Arthur Balfour's Conservative government) was caught off Peate's bowling. It was the start of a devastating spell as only a dropped catch denied Peate a spell of five wickets for five runs. Even so, he finished with 6-14. Yorkshire's innings finished six runs light of Middlesex's total but Peate (4-34) and Bates (6-11) scuttled the visitors out for just 45 to set up a five-wicket victory for Yorkshire.

Peate's next appearance was in the Roses match at the ground which was becoming his favourite – Bramall Lane. It was to result in the sort of victory much beloved in the White Rose acres and restored prestige after the innings defeat at Old Trafford. Lancashire were all out for 87 – Peate taking 2-26 but George Ulyett doing the main damage with 7-32. Yorkshire's response was 353. Even Peate, whose previous top score for his county was just 5, made hay with 23 runs before being stumped. Lancashire made a better fist of their second innings but were all out for 186, Peate recording 4-54 and captain Emmett 5-38.

By the end of August 1879, Yorkshire had completed all their county fixtures. There were still representative matches, such as the Scarborough Festival against I Zingari and MCC to play, but Yorkshire were to field a weakened side. Peate was one of only two professionals to play I Zingari. However, for a young man who had just broken into the county first team and make a name for himself, there was still money to be earned to tide him over the winter. From Scarborough he turned out for Thirsk against an eleven organised by former Yorkshire fast bowler George Freeman, who had retired as a professional but still turned out for sides playing as an amateur. Freeman was devoting increasing time to his business as an auctioneer in Thirsk, near his native Boroughbridge.

Peate was back in action again when he represented the place of his birth, Holbeck, and opening the batting, knocking off 34 runs as they beat Bingley on the Tuesday and then on Saturday he was back with his home town, Yeadon, against Morley. The 'have boots will travel' nature of cricket in this period was evident in his next recorded appearance – this time for Bradford side Idle Lillywhites (they were to drop the Lillywhites tag in 1889) against local rivals Windhill. Peate earned his money as he took eight wickets as Windhill made 73 but his Lillywhites were dismissed for 48 in reply. The Idle club must have thought he was worth the outlay as Peate featured for them again on 27 September against Lascelles Hall. On 7 October he did not have far to walk to Yeadon's White Swan pub for his local cricket team's bowling prize. Even though his Yorkshire duties meant he had only played five times for the club, his 36 wickets at an average of 3.2 brought him the recognition, although it does seem a little harsh on M. Myers, also a professional, who had played 22 times and taken 63 wickets, albeit at an average of 7.15.

At the end of the 1879 season, the 24-year-old Peate could look back with pride and satisfaction upon his breakthrough season. He was still being described in the newspapers as 'the colt' yet he was the county's leading wicket-taker. He had taken 65 scalps at a cost of 719, an average of 11.06. The bowling averages were topped by Allen Hill, whose 29 wickets had come at an average of 6.66. Also ahead of Peate, average-wise, was his spin-bowling twin weapon, Billy Bates, whose right arm-off breaks had brought 61 wickets but having conceded only 656 runs, his average was 10.75. Still, the colt showed how much trust his captain had quickly come to place in him. Nobody bowled more overs than Peate's 663, which was more than 100 ahead of Bates. On the wet pitches of that summer of 1879, he was frequently entrusted with opening the bowling. With bat rather than ball in hand, Peate was considerably less spectacular. His figures of 44 runs from 19 innings was boosted considerably by that standout 23 against Lancashire. His average was 3.2. The *Yorkshire Post* noted ominously that while he was capable of lusty blows, he tended to prefer risk to caution.

With the season over, however, Peate had to get through the winter. His place in the Yorkshire ranks was secure and there would be no shortage of clubs wanting his skills to give them an advantage in the fierce world of local club cricket. However, for now, Peate had to earn his keep. He was still living at home and it seems likely that he was back at the mill. A year later he was to be married but on the marriage certificate he was to give his occupation not as a professional cricketer – a perfectly acceptable, even prestigious form of employment – but as a warp twister. The following year when the census came to be taken Peate had no such doubts. He officially recorded himself as 'professional cricketer'. The days of twisting warp were over.

Chapter 3

Breakthrough

AFTER THE long winter in the mill, Peate was back earning his money on the cricket field as soon as possible in 1880. His first recorded appearance of the season was for his local club, Yeadon, on 17 April. Although he took five wickets, the club lost by three runs to Saltaire. He was back playing for them again a few days later against another Bradford team, Windhill. Peate top-scored with 20 not out and took four wickets but Yeadon lost by four wickets. This was to be the pattern for the summer, playing for Yorkshire but taking full advantage of any opportunity to snatch a bit of extra cash turning out for local clubs.

The opening first-class fixture of the season did not augur well for Yorkshire as they tumbled to a ten-wicket loss at Cambridge University. Peate took only one wicket. An unusual engagement was a match between an England XI and Richard Daft's American XI played at The Oval at the end of May. In truth, this was a money-making exercise as it featured the team Daft had led on a tour to America the previous autumn against an invitational team of leading professionals. The 'American' team included Yorkshire team-mates George Ulyett, Tom Emmett and Billy Bates while Ephraim Lockwood, who went on the tour, acted as an umpire in the game. Peate travelled with them down to London together with another Yorkshireman, Allen Hill, as both featured in the 'England' team. While the fixture itself was fairly mundane, ending in a draw after no play was possible on the first day, it has been accepted as a first-class fixture. More importantly, it enabled Peate to make key connections with other professionals. Among them was Arthur Shrewsbury, the Nottinghamshire opening batsman who had a keen eye for making money from his sport. In the future he was to ask Peate to join a tour of Australia. Interestingly, in 1888 Shrewsbury was to organise a rugby tour of Australia which played Aussie Rules football in Victoria and South Australia.

Another tour that year, one which was tinged with controversy, was that of the Australian team in England led by Billy Murdoch. There was considerable bad blood hanging over from England's trip to Australia in 1879 which had resulted in the so-called Sydney Riot. The incident arose from England's game against New South Wales in February, a month after Australia had beaten England by ten wickets in the only Test of the tour. In truth this was a rather weak English team. An invitation had been sent by the Melbourne Cricket Club to organisers of the Gentlemen of England to send a team out. Lord Harris put together a side but was unable to find enough gentlemen to commit to such a long trip and so he included two professionals – the Yorkshire pair Emmett and Ulyett. The squad was considered strong in batting but weak in the bowling department, especially spin bowling.

Against New South Wales, England followed established practice and picked one of the umpires. Their choice was George Coulthard, from Victoria. England started well and made 237 before the New South Walian innings began on Saturday 8 February. There were 10,000 in the ground and contemporary reports note that a huge amount of gambling was taking place openly despite notices posted stating that it was illegal and would be firmly dealt with by the authorities. Emmett was in top form and the home side were made to follow on, despite their star man Murdoch making 82 not out. It was near the end of the day's play in the home side's second innings when Murdoch went for a quick run and Coulthard raised his finger for a run-out. A combination of the huge bets placed and the fact that an umpire from Victoria, the deadly rivals of New South Wales, had given a controversial decision against them, caused an ugly scene in the ground. There were boos and shouts of 'not out' and 'go back, Murdoch'. The Englishmen stood around waiting for the next batsman to come to the crease – but no-one appeared. Lord Harris walked to the pavilion to find out what was going on and at the gate was met by the New South Wales captain David Gregory. The Australian asked Harris to remove 'his' umpire as he was inept or biased but Harris refused.

While the two captains were arguing over the umpire, a crowd estimated at 2,000 invaded the pitch and began pushing and jostling Coulthard. Lord Harris, who had returned to the wicket, was hit by a stick and the two Yorkshire professionals came to his rescue. Ulyett and Emmett grabbed a stump each and led Harris off the pitch, swinging their weapon at anyone who approached. A.N. 'Monkey' Hornby, a renowned amateur boxer, grabbed one of the assailants and dragged him off the pitch and into the pavilion. Eventually the crowd was cleared and discussions began about resuming the match. The New South Walians at first refused but were told they would forfeit the match if they failed to take the field. When the Englishmen emerged to resume the game, the crowd invaded again. Lord Harris this time stood firm and, according to author Jack Pollard in his book *The Formative Years of Australian Cricket*, refused to leave, standing 'erect with moustache bristling' until the close of play. Fortunately, the following day was a Sunday, a rest day, and tempers had calmed when play was resumed on the Monday. The innings was quickly wrapped up (Ulyett took four wickets in four balls), handing an innings victory to the English team.

The fallout from the crowd disturbances was unequalled until the Bodyline series and caused considerable resentment in English circles. This was, after all, officially the 'Gentlemen of England' team (plus two professionals). The Australians too were unhappy, the *Sydney Morning Herald* describing events as a 'national humiliation' which 'would remain a blot upon the colony for some years to come'. Lord Harris led his team away from Sydney and a second game against an all-Australian side (which would have become the fourth Test match) was abandoned. He wrote to the *Daily Telegraph* stating: 'Beyond slyly kicking me once or twice the mob behaved very well, their one cry being, "Change your umpire." And now for the cause of this disturbance, not unexpected, I may say, by us, for we have heard accounts of former matches played by English teams.' While this played down the incident, he poured fuel on the fire by accusing Australians of being bad losers and not appreciating good cricket.

This then was the background to the Australian tour of 1880, which the English hierarchy considered to have been put together at late notice as purely a money-making scheme. Lord Harris would have nothing to do with the tour, shunning the Australian team and avoiding meetings with them. In his autobiography he was to write: 'They asked no-one's goodwill in the matter, and it was felt this was a discourteous way of bursting in on our arrangements; and the result was they played scarcely any counties and were not generally recognised ... We felt we had to make a protest against too frequent visits.' W.G. Grace (another with an eye for making some money from the game) tried to arrange a match at Lord's but MCC refused to allow their ground to be used. However, the public attitude was quite different and cricket fans flocked to see the tourists. Towards the end of the tour the Surrey secretary C.W. Alcock, doubtless with one eye on the potential gate receipts, asked Lord Harris to put together a team to face the tourists. Harris relented and so the fourth England v Australia Test (and the first in England) took place at The Oval in September of 1880. Three men refused to let bygones be bygones – Ulyett, Emmett and Monkey Hornby.

One county which did not put outrage before income was, not surprisingly, Yorkshire. The Australians had played against Derbyshire but otherwise their fixtures were limited to the likes of St Luke's (Southampton), Longsight (Manchester), Rochdale, Keighley, Burnley and Malton, each fielding 18. Then on 10 June they came to the Dewsbury ground to take on Yorkshire. It was to be the first of many appearances Peate would make against Australia. Emmett (but not Ulyett) were in the Yorkshire side in what was a low-scoring affair, completed in two days. Yorkshire were skittled out for 55 and the Australians fared little better, establishing a first-innings lead of only ten. Yorkshire scored 100 in their second innings, which was not enough to prevent a five-wicket victory for the tourists. For Peate it was a milestone. When he took the wicket of Arthur Jarvis, the 19-year-old wicketkeeper, it marked his 100th in first-class cricket, exactly one year and one day after making his debut. He took 4-20 in the first innings but was without success in the second.

Losing to a side as strong as the Australians was no shame, yet there were accusations that the Yorkshire team had not taken the game seriously enough. A correspondent to the *Sheffield Telegraph* had his letter published on 6 June 1881 in which he accused the Yorkshire side of staying up until the early hours playing billiards or cards: 'If they do not get their proper sleep, no eleven can quit [sic] themselves like men on the morrow. At Dewsbury last year it is commonly reported that on the Friday night they did not go to bed until the sun was up and consequently on the Saturday they lost the match against the Australians.'

Like the previous year, the 1880 season was badly affected by rain. Those conditions suited Peate and his spin bowling partner Billy Bates. Peate recorded his best figures so far with 7-61 against Kent but results were poor. The Roses match was in the balance before the rain intervened and Yorkshire lost to Kent and Notts and then drew with Surrey but the biggest disappointment was a repeat fixture against Australia played at Huddersfield. Once again Emmett played but Ulyett was absent (he did play in the county games which bookended the Australian fixture suggesting that he still bore a grudge). Having won the toss, Yorkshire chose to bat but were out for just 78. The match was abandoned at lunch on day two and there was no play at all on the third and final day, which is probably just as well as the Australians were 229/6. Although Peate only took one wicket, it seems as though he was treated with considerable respect by the Aussie batsmen as he bowled 38 overs of which 22 were maidens, conceding only 31 runs in total. His strike partner Bates took 1-71 while the main damage was done by Ephraim Lockwood, who took 3-29 in 18 overs.

The pressure on maximising a professional's earnings at every opportunity was illustrated when Peate sandwiched in an appearance for his old club Manningham between a rather ignominious defeat to Kent and the Australian fixture. The Kent game had been scheduled for three days but was over in two on Friday, 16 July. Somehow Peate managed to dash back from Maidstone to play for Manningham the following day. Peate would have been committed to playing the third day at Maidstone but Yorkshire's miserable display meant he was suddenly free. There must have been some telegraphic communication between player and club but even so the logistics are quite staggering and Peate would have had to catch a very late train and travelled through the night or a very early train in order to get back to Bradford for the match. Presumably he demanded a high fee but whether it was worth it is open to debate. Peate took three wickets and Bingley were all out for just 38 runs. Peate opened the batting and scored 7 but it was the highest score of the innings as Manningham were all out for 25. More senior Yorkshire professionals such as Emmett, Bates, Pinder and Lockwood stayed in London over the weekend and on the Monday were playing in the Over Thirties v Under Thirties match at Lord's. Peate's reputation was not yet high enough to earn him a place.

There was some hope in Yorkshire circles that Peate could contribute more with the bat. The *Yorkshire Post* commented in August 1880. 'It would appear that the two left-handers Mosley and Peate are rapidly coming to the front as batsmen as well ... it would not surprise us much if Peate improves very considerably as a batter as he plays a pretty straight bat as a rule.' It was, of course, the kiss of death as Peate was out for a duck in his next match. However, he was to score his first-class career-best to date of 27 not out against Derbyshire on 19 August.

As the season drew to a close, the clamour grew for an England representative team to play against the touring Australians, who thus far had played few county sides. As mentioned already, the Surrey secretary Charles Alcock was responsible for adding this match to the itinerary and it is now regarded as the first ever Test match played in England.

Alcock was an innovative sports administrator. He is responsible for the creation in 1871 of the Football Association's FA Cup – and indeed was a player in the first ever team to win the competition, Wanderers. He was also the secretary of Surrey County Cricket Club and he tactfully suggested to Lord Harris, the Surrey captain, that he should defend England's honour and end all doubts about whether this Australian side would beat an English team. There were some who thought Peate stood a chance but in reality, after just two seasons in the county game, he was considered a player with a bit to learn. Even if the call had come, Peate may well have been influenced by the decision of Tom Emmett and George Ulyett who refused to play as a result of the Sydney fracas (though as we have seen, Emmett was prepared to turn out in county games). All three ended their first-class cricket for the season with appearances for Yorkshire against I Zingari at Scarborough. Two days after it finished, the Test started at The Oval.

The first-class season was over, but there was still almost a month of club cricket to play and Peate was ready to cash in on his status as Yorkshire's leading bowler. After competing against MCC and I Zingari at the Scarborough Festival, the Yorkshire team headed to Bramall Lane for a benefit game for George Pinder, who had just finished his career with the county after 13 seasons. Their opponents were 18 from Lascelles Hall, the small village club near Huddersfield which produced many Yorkshire cricketers in this early era, Pinder being among them. The Yorkshire professionals gave their services for free in this game, no doubt with an eye towards their own future when their careers were drawing to a close. The day after the game was over he was back on the field for Manningham, taking seven wickets as Keighley were skittled out for just 50. He squeezed that appearance in between a fixture between Yorkshire County XI and Eighteen of Bradford Albion. This was the sort of match organised locally to raise funds against a strong county team. Although not organised by the county club, it would probably have had the tacit agreement of the Yorkshire secretary Joseph Wostinholm from Sheffield. There was just time before September closed for a game for Idle (Bradford) against Guiseley. One wonders whether Guiseley were delighted to face Peate, whose fame was growing, or put out as he took all ten Guiseley wickets – including two hat-tricks – as they were all out for 19 chasing Idle's 128 (Peate out for a duck).

Another winter, another fallow period for earning. While some professionals found employment at schools, Peate was back in the mills. There was, however, one significant milestone in his life during the close season of 1880/81. On 24 November 1880, Ted was married to 22-year-old Sarah Coultas at Yeadon Parish Church. He described himself on the marriage certificate not as a professional cricketer but as a 'warp twister', a reflection of the fact that this was his main winter source of income. The census taken a few months later shows that he and Sarah were living with her parents, William Coultas (aged 53) and Phoebe Coultas (47) at Gill Lane, Yeadon, along with Sarah's younger brother Arthur Coultas (14), and Polly Hartley, a niece. The marriage was a step up the social ladder for Peate for, in the census, William Coultas gives his occupation as 'cloth manufacturer and farmer of seven acres'. The cloth business must have been a fairly small-scale concern, perhaps renting space for a couple of looms in a larger shed which hosted a number of other similar enterprises. The Coultas family had acquired enough funds to become smallholders as well. Sarah was working as a woollen burler, presumably in the family business, which was a skilled job entailing quality control of the finished product, removing knots and burrs. The younger brother, Arthur, was working as a farm labourer, probably assisting running the smallholding. Ted, however, did not profess to be still in the textile industry. He gave his occupation as 'professional cricketer'.

* * *

The 1881 cricket season began in the cold of early April in a match titled E Lockwood's XI v Eighteen of Hope Foundry and District (Including Ulyett and Peate). Again, this was a fundraiser and quite possibly agreed with the owners of the foundry who took the risk of guaranteeing the three professionals' fees and kept their fingers crossed that the weather would stay kind. Ephraim Lockwood's team was made up of men on the fringes of the county team (for example Joe Ambler was to play for Yorkshire later while David Eastwood's seven seasons with the county had ended four years earlier). It was certainly cold, but the *Yorkshire Post* put the crowd at around 2,000. The foundry team cannot have been relying on Peate to score runs and he made his customary duck, bowled by Ephraim Lockwood. When Lockwood's team came in to bat, Peate bowled exactly half the 42 overs still possible before darkness and took 3-36. However, eyebrows must have been raised and notebooks brought out when a foundry player called Robinson was called on at the end of the day and in his 3.4 overs took four wickets without conceding a run. Alas the second day's play went unreported, crowded out as the newspapers devoted most of their columns to report on the death of former Prime Minister Benjamin Disraeli. Other early-season appearances were recorded. Peate was still turning out for Manningham and also played on Merseyside for a strong United North of England team taking on 18 from Bootle.

The county season started with a victory over Cambridge University, but the next game, a match between Yorkshire and a Colts XXII (effectively a trial match for leading players from across the county) provides food for thought for those who complain about slow over rates and workload in modern cricket. The *Yorkshire Post* reported that the first ball was bowled by Peate at 12.10. By 3.50, Yorkshire were batting as the Colts had been bowled out by Peate and Allen Hill (ten and 11 wickets respectively, the only two bowlers used by Yorkshire). In the three and a half hours of play they had sent down 84 overs – although it must be admitted that these were four-ball overs. It is the equivalent of 56 six-ball overs in well under four hours – including lunch and 22 wickets.

The match against Surrey at Huddersfield at the start of June 1881 possibly gives us our first example of Peate's wayward behaviour that was ultimately to cost him dear. It was an unusual match. Surrey's bowling was weak and they even resorted at one point to call upon their wicketkeeper W.W. Read to bowl 'slow underhands' as Yorkshire piled up what was in those days a huge score of 388 with Ulyett and Lockwood both hitting centuries. What is intriguing is that the innings closed on 388/9 with Peate absent. The cricket statisticians today report that he was 'absent hurt' but contemporary reports mention no injury (and he was to bowl long periods when Surrey were batting). The *Yorkshire Post* commented that he 'was not at the ground on time' and stumps were drawn for the end of the day. The intriguing explanation begs the question, why had Peate not been able to make it from Leeds to Huddersfield at all during the day? There was a frequent service between the two towns and the venue stands on the main line between Leeds and Manchester. On the other hand, was 'not at the ground on time' a euphemism? Could Peate have been nursing a hangover, or indeed had he seen how well the two master batsmen were going and decided to slip out of the ground? As always, the behaviour is inferred rather than publicised.

Whatever, Peate was at the ground the following morning for the resumption of play and showing no sign of injury as he took 14-77 as Surrey were beaten by an innings and 217 runs.

Peate, in common with the bulk of the Yorkshire professionals, was busy this summer. On 10 and 11 June the Yorkshire committee had organised their first ever Gentlemen v Players match which was staged at York. It was a coup for the York club, which had just opened its new ground at Bootham Crescent (later to be the home of York City FC) and aroused considerable interest. Special excursion trains were laid on and the *York Herald* noted that the big attendance was swelled by a large number of visitors from across the county. They were to witness a close match with the 11 professionals beating the 16 amateurs by just 12 runs over two days although it was Hall rather than Peate who did the most damage across the two innings. The perils of booking a top class side for a town club were illustrated later in the month when the North of England XI, including Peate, met the Skipton club which was hoping to boost its funds. They even put up a temporary grandstand in the hope of making an extra 6d from spectators willing to pay for a better view on top of the one shilling entrance fee. Alas for the Skipton club the weather was wet and cold throughout the three days. Play could not start until nearly 3pm on the first day and it barely improved for the remainder of the match and few spectators turned up, play ultimately being abandoned on the final day after just a few overs. Financially, it was a disaster for Skipton, who had to guarantee the fee for the 11 professionals and most probably their expenses. A week later, with a county match against Sussex squeezed in, Peate and the Yorkshire XI were in action again in another of these exhibition matches, this time against a 22 from Ripon. This time the weather favoured the local club and they enjoyed good crowds over the three days. Yet the *Yorkshire Post* noted: 'The attendances were not quite sufficiently large to reimburse the expenses of the projectors of the match. Nevertheless they contemplate another match next season.'

Peate was playing virtually every day in the summer of 1881. If it wasn't for his county it was in benefit matches or for his old club, Manningham. Other than the ones mentioned previously, he was twice in the Gentlemen v Players match at Lord's, for an all-England XI (featuring Peate and Beaumont according to the posters) against an Otley and District 18 and for Yorkshire v Lascelles Hall described as for Hill's benefit. This is a reference to Allen Hill, the bowler who is credited with taking the first wicket in Test cricket, but who was plagued with dodgy knees. Although he continued for another season, the *Yorkshire Post* stated 'the county executive have behaved very liberally towards Hill since his unfortunate accident, allowing him £2 per week whilst incapacitated for work'. The unfortunate accident was a broken collarbone which Hill sustained bowling in Birmingham. In the county matches Yorkshire reeled off convincing wins over Middlesex, Surrey (twice), Sussex and Nottinghamshire but the wheels came off when Lancashire beat them twice in a month with Peate unusually ineffective.

In the end of season review, the *Yorkshire Post* claimed that the first of the Roses matches should have been won quite easily but for too many dropped catches. Peate and Bates were described as the best slow bowling pair in the country and with Hill, Ulyett and Emmett as back-ups, it predicted Yorkshire would have a strong future. Bad weather resulted in the final two county games of the season being drawn and the champions were declared to be Lancashire. At this point there was no recognised County Championship and not all premier county sides played each other. However, the press acclaimed a champion county and Lancashire, with ten wins from 13 games were declared the top side, Yorkshire's ten wins from 16 games being sufficient to be deemed runners-up. Just to show the somewhat haphazard nature of the county game, Lancashire's game against Middlesex, scheduled to be played from 18–20 July, was called off because when the teams arrived at Lord's they found the ground had been booked by Harrow Wanderers and no alternative could be found.

Peate was the leading wicket-taker by some distance with 110 for 1,293 runs, an average of 11.75. His slow bowling partner Billy Bates followed with 72 for 1,090, an average of 15.14 although the best average was returned by Emmett with 9.98 (46 wickets for 459 runs, his average dragged back by giving away 19 wides). Peate batted 20 times and scored 121 runs, the highest being 28 not out, an average of 13.4. His statistics were considerably boosted by that unbeaten 28. The *Yorkshire Post*, however, used this once again as further evidence that Peate would make a batsman: 'It would appear that our former prediction that Peate would eventually train on as a batsman has been amply fulfilled and he may fairly feel proud of the eminent position he has achieved with the bat … the major part of the Yorkshire bowling has fallen on Peate and right well he has acquitted himself as a reference to his figures will testify. On the whole the Yorkshire season has been a brilliant one and the county may well be proud of her representatives.'

Peate's reputation was firmly established and commentaries from the time report on how he was, to use a modern parlance, deadly accurate. Yet the man himself treated any suggestion he could land the ball on a sixpence with some derision. He told Pullin: 'People used to say that I "broke" this and "broke" that but as a matter of fact I never broke the ball much at all. I used to beat the batsman by length bowling, by studying his weak points, deceiving him with pace and flight of the ball and so on. But the talk of "finding a spot" is all "Tommy rot". You must forgive the expression for I really cannot call it anything else. I remember once on a soft wicket it was mentioned that I had bowled one over in which each ball dropped exactly on the same spot. Nothing of the sort; there would be a difference in the pitch of all deliveries, though each might be a good length. It was the elevation that deceived. The balls might seem to drop all on the same spot but they certainly did not; and I could not have bowled on one spot no matter how I tried. Alf Shaw and I have laughed many a time at the nonsense which has been spoken and written about pitching on a spot. Why, it will take a clever man to pitch to a square foot, not to mention a sixpence. There is a length which no batsman can play and I used to study to find it, and also to go for the batsman's weak points. I could break the ball both ways – but very little and I never tried to break it much. For practice purposes we were favourably situated at Yeadon as we were often able to commence practising out of doors in February.'

Chapter 4

The Scandal Tour

IN THE autumn of 1881, Peate could look back on his breakthrough season with satisfaction. With more than 100 first-class wickets he was, by some distance, Yorkshire's leading wicket-taker and had confounded the likes of W.G. Grace with his spin bowling. However, the bleak winter loomed. When an approach was made to see if he fancied the long journey to America and from there across the Pacific to play in Australia with the prospect of earning ten times what he could in the woollen mills of Yeadon, there was no doubt that Peate would opt for the tour. At first it seems he was not in the organisers' thoughts. Australian newspapers in July 1881, drumming up interest in a forthcoming tour, confirmed nine names and said three more from a possible six further players would be chosen. Peate's name was not among the 15. However, Peate's continued strong form throughout the second half of the season and the organisers' wish to send as strong a squad as possible forced him into the final 12.

The thought of an England team touring the United States may seem highly improbable in the modern era, but the side which crossed the Atlantic in 1881 was not the first, nor even the second, to tour North America. In 1859 William

Pickering, a wealthy Cambridge blue who had emigrated to Canada and had been a founding member of the wandering, invitation-only cricket club I Zingari, obtained guarantees of £1,300 from local sponsors with an interest in cricket to fund a tour from England and pay the 12 professionals who committed to the venture a fee of £90 each. They played five matches against local clubs who fielded 22 players and attracted enthusiastic crowds, so much so that Pickering turned a handy profit on his investment. The American Civil War prevented any quick repeat of the experiment but when the Nottinghamshire captain Richard Daft was asked to choose a side to tour Australia via North America in 1879, circumstances had changed. Earlier, cricket had looked like establishing a toehold in the States but the Civil War and the emergence of baseball as another bat and ball sport but one which was over in an afternoon, meant that a cricket tour was no longer as attractive a proposition. Nevertheless, Alderman J.P. Ford, a member of Nottingham Council (who would in 1882 become the Sheriff of Nottingham and who had business interests in the USA), asked Daft to put together a touring side for the autumn of 1879. Daft selected seven of his Nottingham team-mates and asked four Yorkshiremen to join him – George Ulyett, George Pinder, Ephraim Lockwood and Tom Emmett. When they returned to England for Peate's breakthrough season of 1880, there would have been plenty of stories about the lifestyle and easy money to be made. For the young Peate, a trip to the wondrous land of the USA, where the hospitality and sights seemed highly glamorous, was a far more enticing prospect than another winter in the Yeadon mill.

So when a tour was organised to America as a precursor to a trip to Australia in late 1881, Peate needed little persuading to leave behind his wife of less than 12 months and first-born child, Edmund, just a few weeks old. He joined fellow

Yorkshiremen Emmett, Ulyett and Billy Bates in the party invited to head across the Atlantic. The organisers were Nottinghamshire professionals Alfred Shaw and Arthur Shrewsbury (who had both been on Daft's 1879 tour) and James Lillywhite of Sussex, who posterity has credited with being the first captain of an England Test team after winning and losing one match against Australia in 1876/77. Shaw and Shrewsbury had been among the seven Nottinghamshire players who went on strike in 1881 in search of better pay for the professionals. They were to use their time wisely, organising the trip which would eventually net each of them more than £1,500 for their efforts. The offer to each player would see them earn the considerable sum of £300 and there were ample opportunities to top up the basic sum by selling signed equipment and photographs or by paid appearances at dinners, shop openings, etc. It was not a side selected by the cricket authorities and was treated somewhat sniffily in the British press. It almost invariably referred to the team as Shaw's XI as Shaw was the captain; sometimes it was Shaw's XI of England but the authorities and press alike were adamant that this was not an England team. Apart from Lillywhite and one other exception, the tourists were drawn exclusively from the northern counties of Yorkshire, Nottinghamshire and Lancashire. However, the Australians were in no doubt. They generally called the team England or All England. The cricketing establishment took little notice of the tour which had no official sanction (although it was later accorded full first-class status) but the same cannot be said of Australia, where matches were extensively covered in the press with, as we shall see, awkward consequences for the team.

Reports of the Australian tour undertaken by Peate are, to the modern eye, remarkably thin. In the book of excerpts from *The Times* about the Ashes, the editor Richard

Whitehead points out that on the 1882/83 tour (which Peate declined to join), the first Test finished on 2 January but it was not reported back in London until 14 February. Reports would be filed by mail and put on the next available ship home. By the 1895 series, an underground telegraph cable had been laid meaning that play could be reported 24 hours later. In addition, the newspapers relied on local correspondents for these early years and they reported almost entirely on events on the field of play. The antics of a group of young men who were notoriously fond of their ale and seeking amusement was forbidden territory – a situation which might be looked on with envy by later fliers of biplanes, riders of pedalos and aficionados of gambling in touring sides.

Shrewsbury, in many people's eyes the best batsman of the era, withdrew from the American leg of the tour due to a bronchial infection and there was one surprise in the squad – Billy Midwinter of Gloucestershire. He was the other non-northerner but there was a good reason for his inclusion. Midwinter had emigrated to Australia and played for his new country against Shrewsbury's side in 1877. He returned with the Australians on their tour to England in 1878 and was persuaded by W.G. Grace to stay over and play for the county of his birth, Gloucestershire. Selected for the American and Australian tour of 1881/82, he was to play for England (as I shall henceforth refer to them) in the Tests and thus became the only man ever to have played for both Australia and England in Test matches against each other. Midwinter would attract interest (perhaps unfriendly) on his return to the country he now called home and thus boost receipts while, from Midwinter's point of view, it was an all-expenses paid trip back to Australia.

If the London-based authorities and national press looked down their noses at the tour, it was a different story in Yorkshire. It was seen as a great honour to represent the finest cricketers in the North. Before setting out, a dinner in Peate's honour was held at the White Swan in Yeadon on 13 September 1881. His time at Carlisle earned him a reputation as a 'slogger' according to the *Wharfedale Observer* account of the event, although he had now become far more measured. A speech was given by a Councillor A. Lupton from Wakefield, who gave the toast to 'The Health of Mr Peate' and ran through his career in 'eulogistic tones'. Mr Lupton 'had no hesitation in saying that at the present day he [Peate] was the first slow bowler in England and it was an honour to Yeadon that it had produced such a player ... he hoped that the tour about to be commenced would result in further laurels being added to Peate's name and that on his return a right royal welcome would be accorded him'. Peate responded to the toast, but typically it seems as though he was uncomfortable making a speech. The *Yorkshire Post* deals with his response in four words: 'Mr Peate briefly responded.' However, the weekly *Wharfedale Observer* does expand a little: 'Mr Peate said they knew he was no speaker but he felt very gratified in the manner in which the toast had been drank and still more to know that he had the hearty good wishes of his fellow townsmen. He could only thank them for the honour done to him and the good wishes which had been expressed.'

The players gathered in Nottingham for an official send-off and then headed by train to Southampton. Peate was accompanied by his fellow Yorkshiremen George Ulyett, Billy Bates and Tom Emmett. Also invited to tour was Ephraim Lockwood but he pulled out with 'acute rheumatism' although he was to be teased that he preferred to get married. On the trip out to America Peate earned a reputation as a good sailor with an enormous appetite. Tom Emmett, in his interview with Alfred Pullin for the *Yorkshire Evening Post*, said it took 14 days for the ship to get from

Queenstown (now Cobh) in Ireland to New York. He went on: 'For the first seven days we had some sport in the shape of the vessel doing everything but turning over ... While I used to be so ill, Ted Peate was a splendid sailor. He would walk the deck as if ship and ocean were his private property. I was quite envious of him for he would breakfast, tiffin, dinner, ditto repeat and generally have a full time. All the while I was providing the fishes with a liberal supply of provender. I have thought since that after my liberal contributions I should have my fish supplied free.'

Despite the bad weather, the ship arrived in New York on 30 September for a scheduled five matches but it was not to prove a profitable tour for the organisers. The team was in action the day after it landed, travelling by train to Philadelphia to play at the Germantown club, declared to be 'as high tone as the MCC itself'. It was a mismatch. Shaw's team scored 277 and the Germantown club was only able to compile a total of 116 from both innings. Peate was not even asked to bowl in the first innings and then demolished the Philadelphia side with seven wickets from just 103 balls. It was to be a similar story for the rest of the tour with Peate virtually unplayable. The next match, against New York at St George's Cricket Club ground at Hoboken, was equally one-sided, Shaw's team scoring 258 while the New Yorkers were out for 68 and 46. Peate took 14 wickets for a grand total of 65 runs. It was back to Philadelphia for the third game but this time the organisers had decided to try and make things a bit more competitive. The opponents were to field 18 players in a team billed as the United States although almost half were English professionals who now resided over there. After the low attendances at previous matches, this one attracted 6,000 spectators and the attempt to even things up partially worked. The England team scored 114 and 166 while the United States scored 71 and 77, Peate taking 20-61.

The fourth game, in St Louis, was ended by rain before the home side could even bat and from there it was on to San Francisco on 19 October. The *Melbourne Argus* sent out a special reporter to cover the tour from this point and, writing under the pseudonym of 'The Vagabond', he identified Peate and Midwinter as the chief dangers to the Australians. Midwinter, of course, they knew all about but there was much fascination for the new find of English cricket. The Vagabond recorded this final part of the tour in great depth. For instance, he told how an enterprising theatre owner plastered his bills with the announcement that the performance of the play *Alixe* by long forgotten author Alice Darling would be attended by the England cricket XI in the hope that the attendance would be boosted. It wasn't. The Vagabond noted with some glee that the attendance at the theatre was as poor as that at the Recreation Ground in San Fransisco for a match against a local 22 the next day.

'A miserable and mournful place is this Recreation ground, large enough to play cricket in but not to accommodate the thousands of spectators there would be at a match in Australia,' wrote the Vagabond. 'It was as rough inside as outside. The ground was like a stone yard, not even a green oasis near the wickets.' Again, the crowd was disappointing, not 100 people being present at the start according to the Vagabond. He quoted one of the 'colonists' – i.e. an emigrant from the UK – 'I paid a dollar for us to see cricket; this is a farce and it's money obtained under false pretences.' The American bowling was exclusively underarm apart from when a baseball pitcher came on and the England batsmen found it hard to score runs. Lillywhite acted as an umpire rather than played, reducing England to ten men who scored 98 runs. When it came to England's turn to bowl, the wickets tumbled rapidly, prompting the Vagabond to sigh 'it became a dreary farce' as the San Fransisco 22 were all out for 44. 'I don't think anyone really enjoyed themselves except three children who, having any amount of space and benches in the stand to play over, and an unlimited supply of peanuts, took no heed of the game at all.' The match went into a second day when a halt was called with England 322/2. Nobody seemed to care – least of all the professionals– although the Vagabond did his bit to drum up interest by describing Peate as the best bowler in England and predicting that Shaw's team would triumph over both Victoria and New South Wales, but it ought not to be beyond a united Australian XI to emerge victorious. The following day Shaw's XI boarded the passenger ship *Australia* bound for Melbourne.

The *Australia* had one other distinguished passenger – King Kalakaua of Hawaii (then known to the British as the Sandwich Islands). He was the last king of the island, then an American dependency, and was returning home from a world tour. He had a reputation as a fun-loving playboy nicknamed the 'Merrie Monarch' (he is credited with making the famous hula dance a symbol of Hawaiian culture). He found the English professional cricketers splendid company. In his interview with Pullin, Peate reminisced: 'The previous summer he had been in England and some of us were introduced to him at The Oval so that we were quite old pals. King Kalakaua called us into his cabin on board the *Australia* every morning in order to hear Billy Bates sing "My Bonny Yorkshire Lass". At Honolulu we had an invitation to the king's palace. The king offered our ship's captain £300 if he would wait until we could play a match but though Shaw and Lillywhite were quite prepared to play a game to please His Majesty, the captain would not accept the offer.'

After the touring party arrived in Australia Peate wrote home. One of his correspondents was Thomas Blatchley, who owned the chemist shop in Yeadon and was to remain a lifelong friend. Written from Sydney and dated 20 November, Blatchley allowed it to be published in the *Wharfedale Observer* and it gives further insight into the life of these early English cricketing stars. Peate wrote:

'We arrived here from San Fransisco after a very fine passage. It was very hot as we crossed the line [i.e. the equator]. Sleeping below was quite out of the question. Mattresses were placed on deck where we lay with nothing on but shirts and pants. One of the passengers on this vessel was the King of the Sandwich Islands. He had been on a tour round the world. I saw him at The Oval in London where I was playing. He knew me again. When we got on board His Majesty invited us to take cigars and drinks with him in his cabin. We got on very nicely, I assure you. In fact when we arrived at the Sandwich Islands (where I suppose he is "monarch of all he surveys") we had a special invitation to witness his reception at the palace. It was a very grand affair and we were very much amused and impressed with the charming scene. Dusky beauties fantastically arrayed in all the varied colours of the rainbow were here to bid welcome home to his kingship. We were quite taken up with the dancing girls. They seemed to be delighted to see their king again after a long absence. They danced rarely, too; in fact they are considered very fine dancers. But be that as it may, their antics caused us some fun and their king seemed not displeased at their manifestations of pleasure. Arthur Shrewsbury arrived here today. He is better than when I saw him last. Possibly the voyage may do him good.'

* * *

The *Australia* docked in Sydney about 5pm on 16 November 1881. It was a hectic schedule in order to maximise profits. Warm-up games were played against teams of 22 at Maitland, Bathurst, Newcastle and Orange, where the resistance of the locals was described as 'quite farcical in its feebleness' by the *Australian Town and Country Journal*. However, the locals did pull off a surprise victory at Parramatta, considered as one of the best teams in New South Wales. The tourists played their first 11-a-side match against a New South Wales XI, securing a comfortable win, before they headed to Billy Midwinter's new home town of Cootamundra. After what the *Australasian* newspaper described as 'a tiresome journey' (today six hours by train) they arrived late at night in Melbourne where they enjoyed, or perhaps didn't, a champagne reception before taking the field 'as fresh as larks' for a game against Victoria. What all reports agree on was the unusually high level of gambling surrounding the match and the fact that the Victorians were totally dominant for the first three days. They scored 251 with Peate doing best for the tourists with 3-80 off 51.2 overs, almost half of which were maidens. In reply the tourists made 146. Billy Bates, Peate's Yorkshire spin partner who was undoubtedly his superior with the bat but not the ball, top scored with 42. Batting at number one and three, Yorkshire's George Ulyett and Nottinghamshire's John Selby made 2 and 6 before being bowled by Joey Palmer. At the time their failure aroused little comment but after the tour ended it added to a maelstrom of suspicion – as we shall see.

In those days the follow-on was automatically enforced if the first-innings deficit was above 100 and so England went in for their second innings. This time organiser Shrewsbury held out defiantly and made 80 not out as the English side carved out a small lead (for the record Ulyett scored 2 again before Palmer sent his stumps flying although Selby did better with 23). The match was scheduled for three days and England were 162/7 at the close of play on the third day. There was considerable pressure to play to a finish given the large crowd and it was agreed to extend the match to a fourth day. This sparked an even greater flood of betting with odds of 30 to one for an England victory. England extended their score to 196, leaving a target of 94. However, there had been rain overnight and Peate was regarded as the finest exponent of a wet wicket (no overnight covers in those days). In just a few overs Victoria were seven wickets down for six runs and though Harry Boyle led a revival with 43, the Victorians were all out for 75. Peate's figures in the surprise English victory were 6-30 off 31 overs, 17 of them maidens.

In a second letter to Thomas Blatchley published in their local paper, this one dated 30 November and sent from Orange, 150 miles due west of Sydney, Peate gave his views on Australia:

'We seem to be nearly out of the world here. The contrast to home life is very great. The journey here is the finest, as to scenery, that I have ever seen. In crossing the Blue Mountains the line of rails runs on the edge of immensely deep ravines, hundreds of feet in depth. It makes one shudder to look down into the awful depths below. I suppose you will have heard that we have played two drawn games and this one, which we have won. There are some very good players in nearly all the teams here. Cricket seems to be the proper game for them as it is with us at home. One enthusiastic lover of the game played against us here who had actually come 700 miles, 640 of which he performed on horseback, the other 60 by rail. He may have enjoyed the ride here in pleasant anticipation of the runs he would get in the match but the return journey will hardly be as nice as he is sent back with a couple of ducks. Poor fellow, he failed to score in both innings. In the match just concluded I got 12 wickets for 22 runs. We are next off to Bathurst.'

In fact, Peate was doing himself an injustice according to the official statistics. Playing against 22 from Orange and District, the tourists won easily. Peate did not bowl in the first innings but newspaper reports and the Cricket Archive says he actually took 13/22 in the Orange second innings.

The first Test match of the tour, after a fixture against South Australia, was played at Melbourne starting on New Year's Eve 1881 but was most unsatisfactory. Played in front of big crowds exceeding 10,000 on each day it was scheduled to last for three days and was at an intriguing stage when stumps were drawn on the third day. England had made 294 in their first innings, the Australians 320 and England were 238/7 when the umpires called the close of play. Although it was hastily agreed to continue into a fourth day, there was a deadline to close at 3.30pm as the tourists were booked on a ship to play in New Zealand. There was little prospect of any result other than a draw and so it proved. The Englishmen caught their ship having made 308 and having the Australians at 127/3 in their chase of 283 to win. The *Melbourne Age* newspaper said the affair was 'most distasteful' and that future fixtures of this stature should be given adequate time to play to a conclusion. Peate was fairly ineffectual in the match. He took only one wicket, that of last man Cooper, for 64 runs and was wicketless in the second innings. He made 4 and 0 with the bat. The other Yorkshiremen on the tour made a greater impression, Ulyett top scoring for England with 87 and Bates next best with 55.

The tourists rushed from the ground to their ship. After landing at Sydney on 16 November they had played nine matches in 45 days and criss-crossed the southern part of the country. Given decent weather they had attracted big crowds, especially for the state or international matches in Sydney, Adelaide and Melbourne. The New Zealand leg was less popular but even more hectic. They squeezed in victories at Dunedin, Oamaru, Timaru, Waikato and Auckland and drew two rain-affected games at Christchurch and Wellington before dashing back to Australia and two Test matches at Sydney.

Both these Tests resulted in defeats for Shaw's men. For the record, in the second Test England made 133 in their first innings and the Australians replied with 197. England then managed 232 but Australia won with 169/5. It was not a triumph for Peate. While the Australians respected how difficult he was to score from, he took only one wicket in the match. More successful (again) was his Yorkshire rival Billy Bates. There were two quick matches squeezed in in the Sydney suburbs of Stanmore and Windsor before the third Test started on 3 March. Peate did much better in this game. England again batted first and scored 188 but Australia again had a healthy lead with 262. Peate took 5-43 but the damage was done in a stand between Percy McDonnell (147) and Alec Bannerman (70), who took the score from 16/3 to 215/4 before Peate was brought back and snaffled up McDonnell. England were again quickly dismissed for 134 and the Australians reached their target of 63 with six wickets still standing. Peate did best of the England bowlers with 3-15 (plus not out scores of 11 and 8 in the England innings).

Tourist Dick Barlow, in his interview with Alfred Pullin, claimed the players escaped a potential disaster in Sydney although the story is not corroborated by any other player. Barlow said: 'On the 1881 trip we had been out to supper across the river at Sydney and being detained just missed our boat back. It was moving off when we reached the wharf. We were annoyed at our ill luck. But that boat never reached its destination. It was split open in a collision and sent to the bottom and several of those on board found a watery grave. I think Providence must have been watching over us on that occasion.' I have been unable to find any newspaper report about a fatal ferry collision coinciding with the tourists' time in Sydney.

The tourists headed to Melbourne in between the two Sydney Tests, playing a return match against Victoria starting on 24 February and then met Australia for the fourth and last time at Melbourne starting on 10 March. This time they made a better fist of it after again batting first and reaching 309 thanks largely to Ulyett's 149 – Peate chipping in with 13. However, Australia were only nine short after their innings (Peate took only one wicket at a cost of 38 runs) and the game petered out, with England 234/2.

The Englishmen left with a good reputation, the *Melbourne Age* commenting: 'During this visit the Englishmen, whether by their achievements on the cricket field or their demeanour off it, have gained the admiration and respect of all with whom they have come into contact and have always been deservedly popular. Everywhere they have been very cordially received and their receptions at some of the country places have been of a right royal description.' The team had good reason to be in high spirits – the tour had been a highly profitable venture. The *Australian Town and Country Journal* said that gross takings had been £13,000. Expenses had been £5,000, the promoters (i.e. Shaw, Lillywhite and Shrewsbury) had paid their fellow professionals £300 each leaving them to split the remaining £5,000 between them. This account does not reveal if there was a 'bonus' for each of the ordinary professionals, nor does it say how much they had made on the side. There is no hint of any jealousy that the three players who organised the whole thing were paid several times what their colleagues had received. However, £300 was roughly what the players might earn in the English summer. Thus the tour had doubled their income and having a grand time as a hero in the warm Australian climes was much preferable to staying at home with no income, or that of a labourer at best.

The players boarded the *Chimborazo*, a ship powered by both sail and steam, at Adelaide on 24 March for what could be a perilous journey home. Peate, as we have seen, was a good seaman but others were less happy on board. The Australian archives contain a letter to the captain of the ship, J. Ruthven, which shows the long sea journey was far from comfortable. The letter reads: 'We, the undersigned saloon passengers, hereby tender to you our strongest protest against the manner in which the table has been supplied during the voyage and in doing so entirely disclaim any intention of casting blame upon the captain of the ship but we consider that the sending of the ship to sea with as it appears an insufficient or defective refrigeration apparatus and without the proper supply of livestock in the case of any accident happening shows a want of the most ordinary discretion on the part of those whose duty it was to find proper provisions on board the vessel. By the failure of the refrigeration apparatus the most serious risk has been run and it is impossible to contemplate without dismay the consequences which might have arisen to the passengers ...'

The letter goes to request the captain to make the owners of the ship, the Orient Steam Navigation Line, aware of the 'dangers to which we have been exposed by the insufficient arrangements for the victualling of the ship'. There at the end are appended 22 names – not signatures for the letter is all written in the same hand. The very last name on the list is E Peate. He was not the sole cricketer to agree to his name being appended to a complaint expressing dissatisfaction at the food and the prospect of it running out. The letter also bears the names of Billy Bates, George Ulyett and John Selby. Why some but not all of the touring party agreed to their names being added to the complaint is unclear.

One of the passengers, a solicitor from Dumfries called John Wood, appears to have led the case. The company wrote back to him saying the claims were exaggerated. This outraged Wood, who expanded on the claims in his reply:

'Is it not a fact that the Company's advertisements set forth that each ship is provided with an ice house and that an abundance of fresh meat and refrigerated delicacies are provided during the voyage? Now you must know without asking Officers or anybody else that the *Chimborazo* has no ice house and as for the fresh meat you admit the failure. Is it not a fact that the meat supplied during a portion of the voyage was quite unfit for human food? The best answer to that is that it was as utterly unfit that the whole remaining stock had to be thrown overboard and this is not sought to be denied. Is it not a fact that the passengers were put to serious inconvenience in consequence of the failure to supply what was contracted for? This you admit and express regret for. Where then is the exaggeration?'

Wood claims that some passengers were so disgusted that they left the ship at Suez rather than continue on to England. As we shall see, the four cricketing signatories Peate, Ulyett, Bates and Selby were among those to disembark the *Chimborazo* at Suez. The company wrote back to Wood saying they declined to enter into any further correspondence with him and the incident seems to have ended there. It does serve to show that while the tourists may well have been splendidly wined and dined on tour, the journey home was less luxurious.

* * *

If the food provided was a source of complaint and real concern to the tourists, they would soon have other things to worry about. The day after setting off a scandal broke to which Peate was a witness and which was to horrify the upholders of the game's honourable ethos. There had already been rumblings about gambling. The *Sydney Morning Herald* of 4 March 1882 had carried a curious aside about the second match against Victoria played on 24–28 February. On the face of it, it was a straightforward eight-wicket victory for

England. Requiring just 57 to win, Peate was sent in with fellow bowler Dick Pilling to open the batting. Pilling went for 10 runs which brought Ulyett to the crease and he scored just 3, spurning several scoring chances before being bowled while Peate went on to make 33 not out. The *Herald* commented: 'There is one matter in connection with the recent match which should not pass unnoticed. I allude to the performance of Ulyett in the second innings. The fact that a batsman with his reputation should have been at the wicket for over half an hour for three runs made it patent to everybody that some powerful agency was at work. I have heard it rumoured that a certain wager connected with Peate's score had something to do with it. Whatever the cause may have been, the performance was not a creditable one to Ulyett, nor is it likely to raise him in the estimation of either cricketers or spectators.' The *Adelaide Observer* was another to be suspicious, reporting: 'The newcomer [Ulyett] apparently had no desire to score, simply playing balls many of which could easily have been put away.' So, there was talk already of gambling centred around Ulyett with Peate, sent in to bat at number one, possibly involved.

The ship sailed from Australia on 24 March and the next day the Australian papers alleged that two England players had accepted bribes of £500 (a huge sum) to underperform in the very first match in Melbourne against Victoria – the one in which England had followed on but fought back to win. The allegation was that some on the English side had been paid to ensure that bets on Victoria to win were successful (to recap – Victoria scored 251, England 146 and, following on, 198, leaving Victoria a target of 94 in their second innings). The two were named as George Ulyett of Yorkshire and Nottinghamshire's John Selby and the facts had been leaked to the Australian newspapermen as the ship departed (the implication being that one of the team had sought a bonus on his tour earnings by selling the story). The papers also claimed that news of the leak had reached Ulyett and Selby who confronted the whistleblower and a fight broke out on board the *Chimborazo*.

It is important to remember that Shaw's men would have been at sea and unaware of the press coverage when they left Australia. There was a delay at the Suez Canal due to a blockage and, with the dire food provided on the *Chimborazo* already causing dismay, the two accused, Ulyett and Selby, left the party and made their own way home, arriving there before anyone else on 2 May. A second group also decided to make alternative arrangements. That consisted of Peate, Bates, Billy Midwinter, Richard Barlow and one of the organisers, James Lillywhite, and they got back to England on 5 May. The remainder stayed on the *Chimborazo* and got back to Plymouth on 11 May. There was nothing unusual in players making their own arrangements to return from tours, particularly if they wished to get home faster, but the fact that Ulyett and Selby, the two accused of match-fixing, had travelled together to get home first was suspicious. It is possible that news of the Australian allegations had reached England, and a telegram had been sent to Suez and the two wanted to get their story published first.

On 3 May (before any of the other cricketers save his co-accused were back in England) Ulyett issued a statement expressing his horror and utter denial of what was described as a slander and threatened legal action. The *Sheffield Telegraph* reported: 'Ulyett seems to appreciate to the full the importance of clearing the national game of the stigma which such a scandal as that referred to would [have], supposing it had any foundation and so far as he is personally involved in the affair. He expresses a very strong opinion of the conduct of those who are responsible for the circulation of the rumour. Seeing that not only the Yorkshireman's reputation but his very living as a professional cricketer depends upon his ability to prove the utter groundlessness of the charge which has gone the round among all cricketers and the public generally, his repudiation of the whole transaction could hardly be given other than accompanied by a vigorous protest against the action taken by those who have made this, as he regards it, shameful attack upon his character ... He came to the conclusion that the only course he could adopt was to make inquiries to ascertain if possible the origin of the slander and to follow these up by whatever steps competent advice may suggest.'

Billy Bates, in the second group arriving home, said the story was nonsense but on 8 May Ulyett expanded a little in a press interview with *The Sportsman* magazine (Selby appears to have remained silent on the matter). He said: 'It may have arisen out of a little pleasantry at Cootamundra, the place where [Billy] Murdoch lives. There two members of Shaw's team certainly did have a bit of fun (as the Yorkshireman calls it) – that is, they had a set-to ... So far from me having anything to do with the matter, as has been reported, I was the very first to stop the affair when I saw they were losing their tempers.' For a while the matter died down until 24 May when Lord Harris, the Kent skipper and future England captain, had a letter published in *The Times* in which he backed Ulyett as an honourable man (he had been with him on the tour to Australia in 1879) but wanted every player in Shaw's team to sign an affidavit stating that he had performed to the best of his ability in every game in Australia.

It was then that William Wake intervened. A solicitor from Sheffield, he played three times for Yorkshire in 1881 with little success and was later to become a county court judge. His letter, published in *The Times* and also the *Leeds Mercury* and *Sheffield Independent*, posed questions which repeated the claim that Ulyett and Selby had been offered £500 to throw the Victoria match but added that another player, William Scotton, had been offered £250 to do the same. Wake asked was it true that Scotton had turned down the offer, told Shaw and come to blows with Selby and Ulyett? The Cootamundra incident which Ulyett had referred to (and dismissed as a little pleasantry) was a proper fisticuffs and Scotton had written to his father upset at the incident. Wyke claimed that 'the scandal [was] one of the principal themes of conversation' on the *Chimborazo*, that Shaw had admitted that 'something unpleasant' had taken place and that several of the team had indicated that 'there was more "carrying on" (I use their own expression) in Shaw's team than anyone not present would believe'. Wake appears to have inside information; he also treads dangerously, despite being a solicitor, given the unmistakeable threat of a libel action in Ulyett's original statement. Plus, he had been a team-mate of Ulyett's just a few months earlier.

At this point, I refer to the only recorded version Peate ever gave. In Alfred Pullin's book of interviews with former players Peate is quoted: 'There were circumstances connected with Victoria's second innings which I cannot fully refer to …' In other words, Peate is following the old convention now covered by the cliché 'what happens on tour, stays on tour'. As an experienced pro himself, who was not beyond a bit of gamesmanship and earning a few extra pounds on the side, Peate is not going to spill the beans but his very next sentence emphasises his own personal innocence: 'I got two wickets in the first over for nothing,' making it clear that he at least was trying his best to win. He continues to detail his performance, pointing out that after five overs the score was six wickets for seven runs, with Peate taking all six. If anyone had taken a bet to throw the match, they must have been alarmed at Peate's sensational performance. Peate then goes on to say how H.F. Boyle spooned an easy catch to mid-on but was dropped (he doesn't say by whom) and went on to score 43 runs. He does then add a detail which may fuel the conspiracy theorists. The last Victoria batsman, F.E. Allan, was run out by a wide margin (says Peate) and threw his bat down in disgust only for the umpire to say not out. Interestingly, one of the umpires was James Lillywhite. It didn't matter as Allan was clean bowled shortly after and England had won by 18 runs after following on. It must also be said that Peate was not entirely accurate about his performance. When Victoria were six wickets down, Peate had not taken all six to fall. He was overlooking that fact that Billy Bates had taken one of them.

The scandal blew up once the team had left Australia. Here is Peate's version as given to Pullin: 'There was a tremendous amount of betting on the match. The bookmakers were standing up doing business as if they were in Tattersall's ring. We were due to sail to Adelaide and it was said that in order that the match might be finished (it was disrupted by rain) the bookmakers paid the steamship company £300 to delay the boat three or four hours. Sam Grimwood of Halifax, who was living out there, asked me before we started our second innings what chance we had and I told him if the wicket performed as it did in England after rain no team in the world could make 100 runs against us. He then started taking all the extravagant odds against England he could and did so well that he finished up by rushing down to the boat and presenting us with a £10 note each. The bookmakers were very badly hit by the result of the match. Certain of their schemes failed, much to the satisfaction of most of us.'

It is a curious final sentence. What were the certain schemes? And why was the dramatic victory after following on more than 100 runs behind a satisfaction to most, rather than all, of the team?

Following Wake's letter, which reignited the scandal, Ulyett requested a meeting with MCC and on 29 May made an official statement: 'As far as I know, neither I nor any of the team know anything about it. It is not true that any offer of money, as far as I am aware, was made to me or anyone else.' Again, the conditional terms 'as far as I know' and 'as far as I am aware' are more reminiscent of a modern day politician's denial of a scandal than an outraged professional cricketer. Shaw and Selby broke their silence on 12 June with the following declaration: 'We, the undersigned, wish to state, with regard to the so-called cricket scandal in Australia, that we emphatically deny that there is any truth in the rumour that either we, or so far as we know, any other of the team were offered a bribe to lose any of the Australian matches; nor did we hear any such report until after our arrival in England.'

With these declarations the flames of the scandal began to peter out. It became an accepted version (in England at least) that no bribery had taken place but that Scotton and Selby had had a fight in Cootamundra and Ulyett had broken it up. Of course, we are all curious as to what really happened. Malcolm Knox in his book *Never a Gentleman's Game* (2012) says the fight was over a woman. David Frith in *Silence of the Heart* (2001) puts it down to a proposed bribe or 'marital jealousy'. Scotton had separated from his wife before the tour and was to divorce her later in the year.

Ulyett was to tour Australia again in 1884 but Selby's England career was over. In his internet article, Giles Wilcock states that 'a book in the Nottinghamshire cricket library at Trent Bridge contains what was presumably a list of cricketers; next to Selby's name, someone had written "a brilliant cricketer but a blackguard"'. He adds, 'Selby's benefit money in 1887 was instantly swallowed up to pay off his debts and there were questions – including ones of possible criminality – over his finances up until his death in 1893.'

Shaw, the organiser who had denied any crookedness on the tour, published his memoirs *Alfred Shaw, Cricketer: His Career and Reminiscences*, in 1902. He wrote: 'It came to our knowledge that there was a great deal of betting on the result of the [Victoria] match. Most extravagant odds were offered on the Victorian team, in spite of the fact that the weather was wet, and there was a possibility of the home batsmen having to play on a sticky wicket, to which they were unaccustomed ... There were certain influences at work beneath the surface which it is necessary to speak of in order to convey a true version of this remarkable match. It had been hinted to me that two members of our team, both now dead, had received a promise of a bet of £100 to nothing on the Victorians winning. I gave no credence to it at the time I heard of it, but certain cases of misfielding compelled me to come to the conclusion that the rumours were not without foundation. Whatever the scheme actually was, it failed.' This version is similar in part to Peate's but goes on to admit that, on reflection, bribes had been taken. Both Ulyett and Selby were dead when the book was published.

On the other hand Giles Wilcock makes the important point that Selby took two catches in the fateful second innings, including top scorer Harry Boyle for 43 when 19 runs were needed. There were a few dropped catches but England teams Down Under have subsequently had their fair share of poor fielding! Wilcock also states: 'If, as seems likely, Shaw did suspect some of his team of accepting money, why did he not take action? Why did he issue a statement of denial? The answer is probably prosaic. Along with his partners Shrewsbury and Lillywhite, he had ambitions to organise more tours; he would not want his team associated with such damaging allegations. Perhaps self-interest took precedence over morals. Nevertheless, future tours organised by Shaw, Shrewsbury and Lillywhite – of which there were several – featured an agreement with the players which included a penalty clause of £20 for anybody guilty of impropriety or misconduct.'

One other scenario which I am surprised has not been expounded is the possibility that the English professionals were not the only ones taking bribes to lose. All sources express surprise at the vast amount of gambling surrounding the match. The match ended with England 64 runs ahead with three wickets left and so it was agreed to play an extra day. This made all sorts of financial sense for the tourists and the cricket authorities in Victoria but also for the gambling fraternity. With England 30 to one to win on the extra day, eyebrows might have been raised at the Victorians tumbling for 75 and losing their first six wickets for seven runs. True, it had been a wet wicket and conditions were difficult but, as several Australian papers said of the allegations about the England players, there was no smoke without fire.

One of those papers to use the smoke and fire analogy was the *Australasian*. Its edition of 29 April 1882 headlined one article 'The Professional Cricketers of England' and while it stated the paper attached little importance to the rumours of match-fixing, its whole tone suggested the opposite was true. It paints the behaviour of the England party in a poor light: 'We must confess that we are not at all surprised that the bona fides of the English professional cricketers has been impeached and that there are people who believe that, to use a turf expression, some of them have been "got at" … There is too much betting now on the game of cricket and professional cricketers are too frequently seen in the company of bookmakers … On the whole there is no doubt that on the cricket field Shaw's eleven conducted themselves with much propriety … [but] professional cricketers who keep late hours, make bets to some amount, and are seen drinking champagne to a late hour with members of the betting ring when they ought to be in bed must not be surprised if people put a wrong construction on their conduct... Cricketers of note are too frequently watched and shepherded by foolish persons who think it an honour to be allowed to furnish them with champagne and other intoxicating drinks at hotel bars and many a good player before now has been brought to grief in this way. A man cannot play cricket all day and sit up half the night playing billiards, smoking and drinking champagne. He loses his nerve and his eye and if in such a state of depression from an overnight debauch he fails to acquit himself as he should do in an important match, ill-natured persons knowing the company he has kept will shake their heads ominously and draw conclusions not very complimentary to the person concerned ... it was the duty of the English professional cricketers to have kept entirely aloof.' The allegations of staying up all night drinking and playing billiards echo the accusations fostered against the Yorkshire team outlined in the previous chapter.

In England, MCC was horrified at the allegations. It was all too reminiscent of the 1877 tour when Edward Pooley had been arrested in New Zealand over an argument about betting with a local man who refused to pay up (for further details see the books by Rodney Ulyate and Kevin Booth). No wonder it was anxious to sweep the affair under the carpet as much as possible. The tour only added to the low reputation of professional cricketers and Peate was among them – although not implicated in any way by the accusations of betting fraud. However, the reports of drinking, late hours and seedy company were never far behind him for the rest of his career. The Yorkshire team containing Peate (and indeed Ulyett) was to be accused of late nights, drinking and billiard halls. Also to dog Peate over the next years were the allegations that those late nights and drinking sessions would see his performances suffer and his powers wane. This was to have a devastating effect every time he failed to return startling figures with the ball.

Chapter 5

The Ashes

NO MATCH in cricket history can claim to have had the impact of the 1882 England v Australia encounter at The Oval. The echoes of the game will reverberate for as long as cricket is played and clashes between the two countries will forever add to the folklore of 'the Ashes'. The event has become a mystical landmark in sporting history, the basic facts ingrained in even those with only a passing interest in cricket. Those facts are so familiar: how this was the first time England had lost to Australia on their own turf; how this was considered to be the first truly representative England side; how shocked the English sporting public was by the defeat; how a mock obituary notice in a newspaper stating the body of English cricket would be cremated led to the burning of a bail and so the Ashes, probably the sporting world's smallest trophy, was born. And Ted Peate had a pivotal role in the whole affair.

In fact, the sporting notice which appeared on the front page of the *Sporting Times* publication, was not the first reference to the death of English cricket. It was beaten by the *Cricket* magazine which, in the aftermath of the game, published its own whimsical notice stating: 'Sacred to the memory of England's supremacy in the cricket field, which expired on the 29th day of August at The Oval. It's end was Peate.' Although rather clunky, the pun does scant justice to Peate. To the casual observer it pins the blame upon him as the last man out. Yet he had done the bulk of the bowling, tying down the Australian batsmen, and emerged as England's most successful bowler in the match with eight wickets. Certainly, no publication of the time was to pin the blame for defeat on him. Clearly this momentous fixture needs closer examination, some of the myths need debunking and Peate's reputation needs rehabilitating.

Barely had the fourth Test match in Australia earlier in 1882 been completed than the return tour began. Just two days after stumps were drawn in Melbourne the Australian squad to tour England boarded the mail ship RMS *Assam*. It was 16 March and eight days before the England team boarded the *Chimborazo* in Adelaide for their journey home which was detailed in the previous chapter. Just as the English squad found the trip eventful, the Australian trip across the seas was not without its notable features. According to the *Australian Dictionary of Biography*, collated by the Australian National University, after docking in Plymouth on 3 May, the team raced to the Raglan Barracks in the town in order to settle a bet. En route to England the Aussies had been boasting of the strength of George Bonnor, a giant of a man who was 6ft 7in tall and weighed 17 stones and who could, the Australians claimed, throw a cricket ball more than 115 yards. A fellow passenger, somewhat incredulous, struck a bet that he would not do so with his first ball thrown on English soil. Hence the dash to the barracks to resolve the wager where Bonnor duly obliged with a throw of 119 yards. Perhaps using the winnings, Bonnor, his captain Billy Murdoch, Harry Boyle and Tom Garrett then jumped on the train to London while the rest of the squad had to endure a few more days on board the *Assam* before disembarking at Gravesend.

The tour showed that this Australian side was a formidable team and so there was great interest in the game. When they arrived at The Oval they had lost only three of 29 matches – to Cambridge University, to the Players of England (comprising Peate and ten other professionals) and to Cambridge University Past and Present. Selection of the England team was left to four MCC members: Lord Harris, the Kent captain; Frederick Burbridge, the former Surrey captain and now a Surrey committeeman; and two brothers who were part of the family owning the Taylor Walker brewing empire – Vyell Edward Walker, who had played a major role in forming the Middlesex County Cricket Club and Isaac Donnithorne Walker, who succeeded his brother as Middlesex captain. They chose a team of six gentlemen amateurs and five professionals, somewhat surprising perhaps as the Gentlemen had been thrashed by an innings in their game against Australia while their professional counterparts had won their fixture against the tourists – and by an innings.

The five professionals picked were Peate and his fellow Yorkshireman George Ulyett, Surrey's Maurice Read, Nottinghamshire's Billy Barnes and Lancashire's Dick Barlow. All but Barlow had played in that Players' decisive victory over Australia. The six amateurs included five who had played in the Gentlemen's humiliation against the tourists. They were the captain, Albert Hornby, a Lancashire mill owner who also captained England at rugby, W.G. Grace, Allan (A.G.) Steel, another Lancastrian whose family were ship owners from Liverpool, Surrey captain Alfred 'Bunny' Lucas and Charles Studd of Cambridge University. The sixth gentleman was the wicketkeeper Alfred Lyttleton, late of Cambridge University and now of Middlesex.

Whether or not a modern reader might consider the selectors were relying too heavily on amateurs, there was widespread belief that this was just about the best team England could put out. England were choosing from every player who had first-class experience rather than being limited to just those who had taken up an invitation to tour. Only Maurice Read's selection raised an eyebrow on account of his inexperience. The *Manchester Guardian* said it was 'something of an experiment. He has played two or three lucky innings lately, but these do not make a cricketer any more than two or three swallows make a summer.' However, in fairness to the selectors, Read had been the star of the crushing Players' victory. He had scored 130 and shared in a stand of 158 with Billy Barnes as the professionals ran up a first-innings score of 322, which was enough to win the match. He was, in modern parlance, the man in form. The *Daily Telegraph* summed up the consensus: 'Few will deny that their choice is a good one and those decided upon have all merited the honour bestowed upon them.' It also noted that there was not a weak bat among them apart from Peate, although even he did have the happy knack of occasionally running up a good score.

The prospect of seeing England's finest cricketers taking on the Australians drew a huge crowd to The Oval for the first day's play on 28 August. An advert in the *Daily Telegraph* that morning revealed that admission was just one shilling, though to get into the covered stand was 20 shillings and into an uncovered stand was ten shillings. The month had seen rain and dull conditions and the wicket was still wet enough to come in for widespread criticism. An article in the *Athletic News* on 4 August 1930 is perhaps the best surviving eyewitness account. The article is by-lined 'By One Who Was There' and is ended with the author's initials – F.W.P. He claims to have been among the first to enter through the gates and ran to the outfield to grab a place on one of the benches placed around the ground. He had to stay there for ten hours, or the place would be lost, and was fortified by sandwiches and a 'flask of watered claret'.

The Australians won the toss and elected to bat and on the stroke of noon Peate trundled in to open proceedings from the Gasworks End. Right from the start, and throughout the match, the damp pitch made scoring difficult and the fact that only 20 runs came in the first 40 minutes was seen as unusually slow. Bowling from the pavilion end was the other Yorkshireman in the side, George Ulyett, and it was he who took the first wicket with the score on six, bowling Hugh Massie for 1.

The Australians were familiar with the deadliness of Peate's bowling and treated his deliveries with great caution. He would bowl 38 of the 80 overs sent down in the Australian innings and 24 of them were maidens. It wasn't long before he claimed his first victim – the Australian captain Billy Murdoch for 13 with the score on 21. However, it would be the Lancastrian Dick Barlow who caught the eye on this first day. He took a wicket with his second ball, the giant Bonnor bowled for 1, and would end the day with 5-19 off 31 overs. The Australians had slumped to 30/6 with Peate having taken three wickets (opener Alec Bannerman and George Giffen were his other two victims) and Barlow two. Lunch was taken before Jack Blackham and Tom Garrett threatened a bit of a revival. They took the score on to 48 before Garrett was caught off Peate as he tried to force the pace (only one boundary had been scored to date). From there the Australian innings was quickly wrapped up by Barlow for the low total of 63.

The English batsmen found conditions just as testing when they came out to bat at 3.30pm. They lost their talismanic opener W.G. Grace for just 4 and Barlow followed soon after, leaving them 18/2. However, Ulyett and Steel began a partnership of 39 runs, although the *Daily Telegraph*, for one, was not impressed with Ulyett. They criticised him as he 'would persist in running out at dangerous deliveries' and was eventually stumped for 26 with England just six runs in arrears. It was to be the highest score of the innings, but the *Telegraph* noted sniffily that his innings was 'comparatively not a good one'. English wickets continued to tumble steadily with Studd out for a duck. At the time it was considered just one in a string of wickets to fall cheaply but it was to assume possible significance in the second innings. England were 70/7 before, in fading light, Steel and Read tried to force the issue. They took the score to 96 before Steel played on. When Peate was the last man out (for a duck), England had eked out 101 runs with the 'experimental' Read justifying the selectors' choice as he was unbeaten on 19. It was too late to start the Australian innings and so play was halted for the day.

England had a lead of 38 runs and a huge crowd was gathered awaiting entrance to the ground by mid-morning for a noon start. The newspapers put the attendance for both days at more than 20,000, the vast majority of them expecting England to proceed to victory. The *Daily Telegraph* noted that the wicket for the second day was even more in favour of the bowlers but the Australians managed to double their score. Barlow could not repeat his success of the second day and went wicketless while Peate did not have quite the same stranglehold on the Australian batsmen. Even so, he was to finish with another four wickets to finish with a total of 8-71 in the match.

There was an incident during the second innings which has echoes of the Jonny Bairstow dismissal in the second Test of the 2023 Ashes series but this time England were the architects rather than victims of the controversy. It happened when the score was on 114/6 when Billy Murdoch steered the ball to leg and was called for a quick run by the batsman at the other end, Sammy Jones. The wicketkeeper, Lyttleton, fielded and threw the ball to Peate who was fielding at slip. The umpire, Luke Greenwood, takes up the story in a later interview: 'The run was made safely enough and Peate made no attempt to take up the ball. Mr Jones thereupon walked out of his ground to pat the wicket where the ball had risen at the previous delivery and W.G. Grace coolly picked up the ball, walked to the wicket, dislodged the bails and cried "How's that?" Thoms, who was the umpire appealed to, gave him out and out Mr Jones had to go. Mr Murdoch, on seeing what had occurred, remarked, "That's a very sharp practice, W.G.," and to this day I think it was. Had I been appealed to I should not have given Jones out, for the ball was to all intents and purposes dead and there had been no attempt to make a second run.'

Apart from Murdoch's cutting remark, there was no protest from the Australians but some in the crowd booed and voiced their disapproval. Many newspapers made little of the incident and *Wisden* had this to say: 'Several of the [Australian] team spoke angrily of Grace's action but the compiler was informed that after the excitement had cooled down a prominent member of the Australian XI admitted that he should have done the same thing. There was a good deal of truth in what a gentleman in the pavilion remarked, amidst some laughter, that "Jones ought to thank the champion for teaching him something".'

It was not the only accusation of gamesmanship. In his 1930 article the eyewitness 'F.W.P.' wrote: 'This is the game in which it was roundly asserted that Spofforth had cut up the pitch by dragging one foot when running on after delivering the ball. I prefer to think it was unintentional though it is true that only after changing from gasworks to the pavilion end did he begin to skittle out our batsmen. Up to the time he changed over, England seemed in little or no danger.'

The Australians owed much to their top three batsmen for their total of 122, in particular Massie, who top scored with 55. He was dropped by Bunny Lucas from a relatively easy catch off Barnes when he was on 38. Those extra 17 runs were to prove critical. Murdoch made 29 but the only other to make double figures was opener Bannerman with 13 as the Australians went from 70/2 to 122 all out.

England needed 85 to win and, despite the wet wicket, overcast skies and occasional shower, they were widely expected to get them, albeit with a few scares along the way. However, the great Australian Fred Spofforth, who was frequently referred to in the newspapers as 'The Demon Bowler', was to write his name into immortality by following up his 7-46 in the first innings with 7-44 in the second and win the match for his country. In that 1930 article eyewitness 'F.W.P.' relates a moment of levity in the match. Dickie Barlow, the Lancashire batsman who came in at number three after the dismissal of the captain Albert 'Monkey' Hornby, was preparing to face Spofforth and was yet to score. Three times he took guard, twice leaving his crease after doing so in order to pat down some of the wicket. At the other end Spofforth had been waiting patiently, tossing the ball in his hand. Twice as he was about to launch his run-up only to be stopped by Barlow holding up his hand and attending to his pitch repairing. On the third occasion of him taking guard, Barlow slapped his chest and swung his bat 'windmill fashion' and indicated he was ready. Spofforth charged in and sent the stumps flying for a golden duck. 'This was rather serious but the crowd simply had to laugh,' said 'F.W.P.' 'And laugh we did with spontaneous unanimity.'

Despite the early scare of losing Barlow without scoring, an upset still did not seem on the cards as W.G. Grace and Ulyett steered England ever closer to their meagre target and reached 51/2. However, with only 34 to get, the Englishmen had a collective failure of nerves. Even so, when England needed just 20 more runs they had Lyttleton and Lucas at the crease and Steel, Studd and Barnes, all considered competent batsman, to come in before the last man Peate.

What followed was a classic collapse all too familiar to England supporters across the decades. From 66/4 England crashed to 75/9 and it was time for Peate to walk to the wicket and into cricketing legend. At the other end was Charles Studd, who was yet to face a ball. The fatal over was bowled by Harry Boyle, a medium-pacer who had removed Bunny Lucas with his first ball. It was widely expected that Peate, the renowned batting 'rabbit', would try to see out the remaining three balls (these were the days of four-ball overs) and leave it to Studd to try to see England home. Instead, Peate turned the first ball he faced to leg for two runs. The next was defended but then, off the last ball of the over, Peate tried to hit out but missed and his stumps were knocked over. Cue the recriminations.

The common view is that English sporting circles were horrified and English cricket gripped by a crisis of self-doubt. In fact, the following day the newspapers were remarkably sanguine about the defeat, an attitude perhaps best summed up by the *Daily Telegraph*: 'The crowd would rather the victory had gone the other way but were generous enough to admit that our visitors had fairly won and by means of splendid cricket ... a contest fought with indomitable pluck by the visitors.' No-one could deny that this was the best team England could have put out. For the first time the best players were available and had been hand-picked by men who knew the game. This was not an England chosen from the best players who had opted to tour or were restricted by qualification in categories such as the North, the South, Gentlemen or Players. However, it was seen as a freak result, due more to the poor wicket than to Australian superiority and there were several calls for a rematch to be fitted into the hectic tourists' schedule, where a better wicket would produce a truer representation of English batting superiority.

A second reason for the defeat was the poor batting of the England team and newspapers hinted at a lack of moral fibre. For example, *The Sportsman* was one of the most dismissive of English frailty. It said: 'How came it then that out of such an eleven only four were able to reach double figures? Whilst in their second venture – well it might be advisable to drop a veil over the second if that were possible but under the circumstances it is not ... W.G. Grace played up like a man ... he was ably seconded on what there is no wish to disguise was a bad wicket by Ulyett but as to the rest, with the exception perhaps of the Hon. A. Lyttleton, they simply collapsed. When the close drew near and their task was but a light one, they simply lost their nerve and stood up to be knocked down like so many ninepins.' Its summary was: 'They were like tailors' dummies ... the closeness of the finish was too much for their poor nerves.'

Wisden too was unable to explain the batting collapse as it analysed the relative statistics of the two teams: 'It will be observed that in every instance the batting average of each member of the Australian team is lower than that of the English batsman placed opposite him, and that the bowling averages of the two men who had the largest share of the trundling for England are both better than either of those of the two bowlers who sent down the largest number of overs for Australia. A perusal of these statistics must in the first place create a feeling of surprise that when the two elevens met there was the slightest probability of the English one being defeated. Secondly, no sensation but one of the highest admiration of the achievement of the Australian team can be felt when the result of the match is considered;

and thirdly the figures prove, if figures prove anything, that the inevitable result of a series of encounters between the two elevens would be victory for the Englishmen in a very large proportion of the matches; and they further offer the strongest protest to the oft-raised cry of the decadence of English cricket.' Its conclusion was that the result was down to four factors: the Australians winning the toss and thus having first use of a wicket which was to deteriorate in the wet weather and play into their hands; secondly the way Spofforth had saved one of the performances of his life for this match; thirdly the nervousness of the England team; and finally the 'glorious uncertainty of the noble game'.

One thing common to the newspaper reports was the performance of Peate in the entire match and Barlow in the first innings. They had emerged from the game with their reputations intact and could hold their heads high. This made the hugely influential *Cricket* magazine's jibe that English cricket supremacy was over and 'It's end was Peate' all the more cruel. Another common theme was the way the Australian victory had been greeted by the crowds. It was a true example of British standards of fair play and appreciation of a plucky victory by gallant underdogs who had seized their chances. The *Illustrated London Daily News'* verdict was: 'There is no doubt that the colonists had a little better luck in the shape of wickets and light than we had but they fully and thoroughly deserved their victory. They played an apparently hopeless game in the most marvellously plucky fashion; and though we know well that it is far easier to save runs than to make them, our men could not possibly have lost if they had displayed one tenth of the determination shown by their opponents.' If any commentator did demur from the view that Australia had just got lucky it was the correspondent of the *Manchester Evening News* who wrote: 'The result was a question of play, not of luck, and we must not begrudge the Australians their victory. They are a splendid team who always play good cricket and though they carry away with them a lot of money, they always leave behind good money's worth.'

Soon, however, the focus turned away from Australian pluck and Spofforth's heroics and back on the feeble effort England had made in chasing down such a small total. *Cricket* magazine was scathing: 'Spofforth's bowling was extraordinary, no doubt … too much cannot be written in praise of his bowling at the critical time but even this will not explain the utter failure of England's last batsmen. The play was irresolute to a degree. Ball after ball of Boyle, some of which might certainly have been hit, passed by unpunished by players who have hitting powers. In fact our batting utterly failed when an effort was wanted.'

The newspapers split into two camps: those who condemned the England batsmen and those who praised the Australian performance. Pitted against *Cricket*'s dim view, the *Athletic* newspaper spoke of 'dastardly attacks' in the press against players whose only fault was that they had not been able to achieve success: 'We have been told with sickening iteration … that this unaccountable collapse was due to the possession by the English players of that undesirable ornament known as "the white feather". A more infamous and unjustifiable accusation was never made against any body of men and it comes with a particularly bad grace from people who, only a few days before, could hardly find language fulsome enough to sing the praises of the men they now accuse of cowardice.' *Athletic*'s view was that if the two teams were to play again a dozen times the same outcome would not be repeated – that was the wonderful thing about cricket – the unexpected could and did happen.

* * *

It was at this point that a young journalist called Reginald Shirley Brooks placed an advertisement in the form of a death notice in the *Sporting Times*, a paper he wrote for. It was to be probably the most famous death notice in the history of newspapers: 'In affectionate remembrance of English cricket, which died at The Oval on 29th August 1882. Deeply lamented by a large circle of sorrowful friends and acquaintances. RIP. NB — The body will be cremated and the ashes taken to Australia.'

Brooks was an archetypal scurrilous journalist whose father had been the editor of *Punch* magazine, a satirical newspaper which was well read in higher society circles. Indeed, at the time of his spoof obituary, Brooks was writing for *Punch* but either he or the magazine considered it inappropriate for them. Instead he placed it in the *Sporting Times*, another publication he wrote for. According to Alexander Andrews' *Chapters in the History of British Journalism*, the paper thrived 'less upon its racing news than upon its profusion of coarse and scurrilous scraps of tittle-tattle'. Brooks himself was, according to author Simon Briggs, 'a stereotypical boozy hack who chased actresses, gambled recklessly and drank himself to an early grave'. Brooks became a legendary figure among tabloid journalists, a favourite story being that when the weekly *Sporting Times* was going to press it was found to be three columns short of copy and Brooks and his colleagues were too drunk and too lazy to write anything to fill the space. The problem was solved when Brooks simply cut out a lengthy article from a magazine called *Truth* (a sort of *Hello!* of its day) and sent it down to the printers to be copied in full and run under the headline 'How on earth did this article get published in the columns of *Truth*?'

So while the source of the momentous Ashes legacy was undoubtedly perceived as a rather crass joke, Mike Selvey uncovered a somewhat more serious background to Brooks' action. In a 2009 article in the *Guardian*, Selvey explained that Brooks' father had been a firm advocate of cremation as a means of disposing of a dead body. At that time, cremation was illegal and Brooks Senior's hopes of a cremation when he died in 1874 were thwarted, his body being buried at Kensal Green cemetery. However, in 1882, the issue came to the surface again when a Dorset military man called Captain Thomas Hanham sought the help of the Cremation Society to dispose of his wife and mother, whose bodies were being housed in a mausoleum. The Home Secretary rejected the Cremation Society's approach for permission so Captain Hanham simply built a furnace on his land and went ahead with the cremation. The Home Secretary wisely declined to take any action. The case was a huge cause célèbre in 1882 as The Oval events were taking place and the journalist Brooks must have followed the case closely, having been fully aware of his father's passionate advocacy of cremation. Hence the topical reference to cremation and ashes in Brooks' death notice. 'He was not being twee at all. Unable to accord his father the funeral he wished, he promoted the cause through his notice,' said Selvey.

As the months went by, the cricketing world started to seek better answers to the riddle of England's defeat. Dickie Barlow, interviewed by Pullin 16 years later, blamed the captain, Hornby, for taking the field too early on the second day. Heavy overnight rain had fallen and Barlow clearly believed the captain should have pressed for a delayed start: 'The ground was wet, Peate and I could not stand while the ball was like soap. I had to get the groundsman to fetch a spade to get the mud out of the bowling holes so that I could fill them up with sawdust ... I ground my teeth with vexation time after time; and if I ever swore in a match – to myself – it was then.' Barlow, who had been the most successful

England bowler in the first innings, went wicketless in the second as the Australians made their match-winning 122 runs. George Ulyett, in his interview with Pullin which took place just a few months before his death, blamed the lower-order batsmen. Typically, he says he was never nervous when he batted and with W.G. Grace took part in a stand of 43 in the chase for just 85. However, when he was out, 'I am afraid that one or two of our batsmen were a bit nervous ... they let Boyle bowl maiden after maiden when a hit or two would have made all the difference.'

Attention began to focus on Peate's swing and miss which had completed the Australian victory. Why, the cricket world began to ask, had he not simply played defensively and let Charles Studd, a recognised batsman, take the responsibility of scoring the few runs still required? It was a question that was to dog him for the rest of his career. Peate himself said he was not nervous and pointed out that four batsmen failed to score a run – if they had scored just two runs each like he did then England would have won! He is supposed to have been instructed by Hornby to keep his wicket intact to let Studd do the business and, on returning to the pavilion, told his captain 'I couldn't trust Charlie.' W.G. Grace in his autobiography commented: 'Not a bad remark, considering that Mr Studd had made a hundred against the same bowling a month or so before.'

Studd was a complex character. He had been Lord Hawke's captain at Eton and they had played together as stars of the Cambridge University side. After graduating (in the year after The Oval defeat) he played for Middlesex and was to score 4,349 first-class runs at an average of 30.49 with eight centuries. Then, in 1884, he gave up cricket entirely to start missionary work in first China, then India and finally Africa, where he died at the age of 70. Along the way he gave away his £29,000 inheritance to be used for Bibles, missionary work and the Salvation Army in England. When picked for England he was only 22 years old but not inexperienced, having played regularly for Cambridge and Middlesex. It is possible that he was a bag of nerves when called out to the middle in an England crisis. However, there are others who deny that he was in any way apprehensive having made two centuries against the Australians already that summer.

Tellingly, Studd went in at number ten. In the first innings he had gone in at number six and made a duck. Is it possible that even his captain had doubts about his mental state? Although, it must be said that Hornby had batted at number ten in the first innings but went in as an opener in the second – batting orders were considerably more flexible in this era. In fact Studd was not to face a single ball, coming in when a wicket fell to the last ball of the penultimate over. His 1934 biography by Norman Grubb quotes him: 'Hornby on his own account began to alter the order of going in. He asked me if I minded and I said, "No." Then things began to change and a procession began. Of course Hornby told me he was holding me in reserve. So I went in eighth and saw two wickets fall and myself never received a ball.' Again, memory has played its tricks as all accounts say he went in tenth.

Peate, in his interview with Pullin, tells how he had been asked (again) why he did not let Studd take on the responsibility and replied 'Quite honestly, I thought I was the better bat!' He adds that Charles Thornton – the founder of the Scarborough Festival, another ex-Cambridge man who also played 200 first-class matches mainly for Kent, Middlesex and MCC – backed him up on this. Peate told Pullin: 'Mr C.I. Thornton then chimed in, "Yes, you're quite right, Ted. Before they went in Charlie was walking round the pavilion with a blanket around him; Steel's teeth were all a-chatter and Barnett's teeth would have been chattering if he had not left them at home."'

That is not the only evidence that Studd was struggling to compose himself. The account written by 1930 eyewitness F.W.P. in the *Athletic News* had a sub-heading which stated 'Peate was RIGHT' with the final word in capitals. F.W.P. said: 'I think Peate was fully justified in going for the forlorn hope in the circumstances. Grand a bat as "C.T." [Studd] undoubtedly was … he was palpably a bundle of nerves while standing idly at the wicket. It was on that account I believe that he went in very late – tenth if I am not mistaken. Anyhow, I remember he did not receive a single ball.' Peering through binoculars, the author says he was 'chilled to see how plainly each was wearing the same "hopeless dawn" expression and how nervous, dejectedly, each man took up position … Peate's "wild pull" at his first ball from Boyle was nearly a fourer. Tommy Garrett fielded it just in front of the sitters-out in front of where I sat. It brought the first cheer for an hour and the first run for 20 minutes! The Yorkshireman shaped to hit the next one over our heads. A mighty swipe. But alas! The ball met unresisting air; the ball hit the stumps – and there we sat, silent, stunned, looking at one another in mute misery save for one hoarse whisper in awed accents, "Gawd. England's beat." Then a wonderful thing happened. Recovering from the momentarily stunning shock of defeat, thousands leapt to their feet with ringing cries of "Well played Australia!" Surging round the pavilion, the crowd cheered the winners again and again. This quick reaction from the depths of gloom and humiliation from this, the first shattering blow to our insular pride, was a revelation.'

The author of the eyewitness account, writing about events which had taken place almost half a century ago, pins the blame on England's defeat on another person – A.P. 'Bunny' Lucas (yet another Cambridge graduate). F.W.P. says the catch off Massie went straight to him and was a simple one. Massie went on to score 55.

He also sheds another mystery on legends surrounding the game. Many subsequent accounts of the match state that the tension was so great on the final day that one spectator suffered a heart attack in the final over. According to the *Daily Telegraph,* 'immediately after the conclusion of the Australian innings', George Eber Spendler, of 191 Brook Street, Kennington, felt unwell and fell to the ground with blood coming from his mouth. He was taken into the pavilion but declared dead due to a ruptured blood vessel. However, F.W.P.'s account is somewhat different. According to him the death happened at lunchtime on the second day, when, as Ulyett and Grace appeared to be steering England to victory, a middle-aged man close to him and wearing a frock coat tried to get near to the pitch where some were sitting by the rope but tripped: 'A minute later there was a call for a doctor. Someone shouted, "Fetch Dr Grace, he's not gone in yet." Soon followed the burly doctor wearing his Zingari blazer. Another doctor also. A brief examination and then the verdict: "He's dead, bring the body round to the back of the pavilion," sounded almost callously casual to the awed onlooker.' According to F.W.P., the story that he died at the conclusion of the match at 6pm is simply incorrect, an account backed up by the *Telegraph* although it has a different time for the fatality.

The wonderfully evocative description of Ashes for the England v Australia contests might have withered on the vine after the appearance of the spoof advertisement in a low circulation magazine. However, in what *Wisden on the Ashes* describes as 'a throwaway remark', the Hon. Ivo Bligh remembered it when he took a party on tour to Australia at the end of 1882. Some say he told a welcoming reception held in Melbourne that his team were there to recover the Ashes. Simon Briggs, in his book, *Stiff Upper Lips and Baggy Green Caps*, sheds a more Australian perspective on the birth of the Ashes. He writes that Bligh's England team were on the same steamship as the president of the Melbourne Cricket Club, Sir William Clarke. As Briggs puts it: 'Relations had become quite cordial, especially between Bligh and the Clarke family's music teacher, the beautiful but low-born Florence Morphy.' The Clarke family were wealthy landowners around Ballarat and Sunbury to the north of Melbourne and owned a mansion called Rupertswood which was so large that it even had its own private railway station and it was here where the Hon. Ivo, the heir to the earldom of Darnley, would hurry whenever the cricketing schedule allowed. At Christmas in 1882, Clarke's wife Janet and Miss Morphy presented Bligh with a red clay urn just four inches high containing the remnants of a bail (or a ball in some recounting) as a joke. Inscribed on the side was the doggerel:

> When Ivo goes back with the urn, the urn;
> Studds, Steel, Read and Tylecote return, return;
> The welkin will ring loud, the great crowd will feel proud,
> Seeing Barlow and Bates with the urn, the urn;
> And the rest coming home with the urn.

The courtship of the England captain and the music teacher continued and in 1884 Bligh returned to Australia to marry Florence Morphy at Rupertswood. The couple returned to the Bligh seat in Cobham, Surrey, and in 1900, upon the death of his father, Bligh became the Earl of Darnley. As for the tiny urn, it remained in the family's ownership until Ivo Bligh's death in 1927. Lady Florence presented the trophy to MCC, where it has resided ever since.

* * *

If the English press had greeted the defeat at The Oval with bemusement, rather than anger, what of the reaction of their Australian counterparts? At first, the news was greeted with a muted response. However, that was due to the fact that no

Australian newspaper had the resources to send their own correspondent across the sea for months on end in order to give an Antipodean viewpoint. The media relied solely upon syndicated reports from English journalists working for news agencies such as Reuters. They stuck solely to descriptions of wickets falling and their comments are limited to praise for the Australian fighting spirit, the quality of their fielding and, of course, the skill of Fred Spofforth.

However, it did not take long for the victory to assume larger proportions. It began to be portrayed as a sign that the Australian nation had come of age. Witness this from the *Sydney Daily Telegraph* which, three days after reporting the win in sober terms, went into patriotic overdrive: 'The All-England team contained some of the finest players in the United Kingdom. What batsmen are there to surpass Grace, Hornby, Lucas, Lyttleton, Studd, Steel and Ulyett? And we suppose that Peate is now recognised as the best bowler in England. But the Australians were more than a match for this tower of cricketing strength and the English papers give them every credit for their victory which they admit was thoroughly well deserved ... Their numerous victories will help to confirm the impression that the Anglo-Saxon race is developing a finer physique in the colony than at home, will set people thinking about Australia and we shall not be surprised if it leads numbers of stalwart young men in the counties of England to resolve to emigrate to the lands which can produce such fine cricketers as we have sent to the mother country.'

The sentiments were catching and the *Brisbane Courier* caught the triumphalist bug: 'In conclusion, it is well that Australia has won nearly all her cricket matches in England; it will bring the new country to notice and save it from being despised as of yore; it will set England thinking and make her look to her athletes and try to do in England what her sons can do in Australia ... There can be no jealous rivalry; we are far more English in feeling than ever was America even before the revolution of 1776 ... We can beat, or be beaten by, England on the fields of peaceful rivalry and bear both fates with uniform friendly goodwill. We are one people and cannot be divided among ourselves.' The *Queensland Times* crowed that Australian batsmen were the equals of the English but their bowlers were indisputably superior. It continued: 'It appears to be admitted that Australians are superior in pluck and determination and this is the greatest compliment that could be paid them. We sincerely hope that after this magnificent victory there will be an end to all those silly and unpatriotic attempts to decry and ridicule our colonial cricketers. They have proved themselves at least quite equal to any that can be produced elsewhere and once and for all let that fact be admitted here as well as in England.'

Talks of racial brotherhood and friendly rivalry could be quickly upset. Most newspapers, including many of the smaller provincial publications, picked up a syndicated report which quoted an unnamed paper published 'in the south of Scotland' which had printed an unfair denunciation of the Australian team. The report, identical in all the papers, accused the British publication of writing: 'The tour of the Australian team of cricketers, excepting that they are making a good deal of money, seems to be a very unpleasant one. Wherever they go there is a difficulty and something very like a brawl and by the time they have completed their visit the interest of cricket in this country will have been considerably damaged. Two years ago, before they left us they offered with apparent generosity to play at The Oval for a benefit match. At the last moment, however, the question of terms cropped up and there was trouble after which it was not expected that they would be starring in England again. They are very much hurt and disappointed to find that they are not feasted and feted as hitherto. Not that they have occasion for complaint ... This week they are to play at The Oval where, no doubt, they will make it a grievance if Lord Harris does not provide them with beds and look after their washing.' The article was greeted with outrage across Australia. So, in 1882, just as on the pitch the great England v Australia rivalry had risen to new heights, so had the two nations' press limbered up and was ready to stoke the fires of Ashes battles.

* * *

What is remarkable is the number of times Peate played Australia in this calendar year. As well as the four Test matches in Australia at the start of 1882 and the one at The Oval, Yorkshire played the tourists five times. In addition, he was in action against them in four further representative matches. This made a total of 14 matches against Australia in the calendar year but it could have been even more as Peate should have been in action against them at his Holbeck birthplace on 11 September playing for Shaw's XI (i.e. the team which had toured Australia a few months previously) but he suffered a sprained ankle when he jumped from a Hansom cab and his place was taken by James Lillywhite. However, he was picked for the victorious North of England side against Australia at the end of the same week. *Cricket* magazine states that 'the Northerners were mostly indebted to Peate for their triumph. His bowling fairly puzzled the Australian batsmen and he has never bowled with more remarkable precision. The ground did not help him in any way but he took five wickets in each innings and in all his ten wickets only cost an aggregate of 105 runs.' His performance was all the more remarkable as newspaper reports make clear he was barely able to hobble due to the sprained ankle. It was also one of his better batting displays as he scored 29 not out batting last in the North's total of 245 and then he set up a ten-wicket victory for his team as he took 5-54 in the Australian first innings of 110 and 5-51 in their second innings of 162. The *Athletic News* commented: 'On a wicket that was all against a slow bowler, he kept such a wonderfully good length that over and over again he beat the batsman and he certainly had hard luck in not getting even more wickets.'

The tourists aimed to squeeze every last penny from their trip and another match against Shaw's XI was arranged for 18 September (in other words straight after the North of England game) at The Oval. Peate continued where he left off. According to *Cricket* magazine, he was still suffering from the sprained ankle injury resulting from his cab accident in Leeds: '[the Australians] were fairly puzzled by Peate who, though very lame, has rarely kept a better length'. With this game concluded, the Australians were heading north again for the 38th – and final – game of their tour against an England XI at Harrogate. The England team should have been captained by W.G. Grace but he backed out due to 'professional engagements' and former Yorkshire captain Ephraim Lockwood was in charge of the side. *Cricket* magazine reported: 'The team was not a particularly strong one but it made a good fight chiefly thanks to the bowling [this is an error – the reporter clearly meant batting] of the Hon. M.B. Hawke, Emmett and the effective bowling of Peate.' However, the locals were not quite so sure. Peate was still suffering from his ankle injury and was 'by no means up to his old form and was probably glad to hand the ball over to Ulyett' according to the *Yorkshire Post*. That seems a bit harsh as he took four wickets in both innings.

There was one incident in this game, described in his book by Pullin, which again echoes down the decades foreshadowing the Jonny Bairstow incident. In the England

XI's second innings Peate, batting at ten, was going along nicely with 14 to his name. Alec Bannerman, fielding at cover point, noticed that Peate was wandering out of his crease after playing his shot. For a few balls he tolerated this but when Peate wandered out even further he threw the ball rapidly back to wicketkeeper Jack Blackham, who knocked off the bails and appealed successfully for a run out. 'Never before or since has a batsman seemed more utterly crestfallen than Peate appeared as he walked to the pavilion amidst the laughter of the crowd,' said Pullin. 'The only persons who did not laugh were Peate himself and little Alec, whose "dander" was up to such an extent that his moustache fairly bristled.'

His other appearance against the Australians had come at The Oval starting on 10 August, for the Players' XI (i.e. a team made up exclusively of professionals and under the captaincy of Ephraim Lockwood) when the tourists suffered an innings defeat, Peate taking five wickets in the match and cementing his place in the England team for The Oval, if there had been any doubt beforehand.

If Peate had suffered embarrassment at The Oval, it was a rare setback in what had been a fabulous season for him. In his interview with Pullin, he was to nominate 1882 as 'undoubtedly my best year with the ball'. He finished the season with 165 wickets which he was proud to relate was the best ever performance in a season for Yorkshire. He was to go to his grave still holding the record despite both Bobby Peel and Schofield Haigh coming close to toppling him. That summer of his death, the record was broken by Wilfred Rhodes.

However, the domestic season had got off to a bad start for Yorkshire. The *Yorkshire Post* described them as downhearted and crestfallen after being 'chopped up', by MCC and Nottinghamshire. The Notts result was particularly galling as they had lost their last five wickets for just one run.

Choosing its words carefully, the article continued: 'After the weakness exhibited by Yorkshire so far, letters are being published recommending the Yorkshire executive to infuse new blood into the ranks,' and the newspaper highlighted just who it meant, the Honourable Martin Hawke. It wasn't so much a criticism of the talent of the current team, it was the suggestion that they were too cavalier, too lax, in modern parlance too unprofessional to turn the talent into results and the *Yorkshire Post* thought it had the answer: 'There are several first-class amateurs in the county and it would doubtless give general satisfaction to Yorkshiremen if they were asked to play in some of the important county games'.

The professionals bucked their ideas up with a convincing win over Derbyshire and then an honourable showing in two matches against the touring Australians. In the first, a rain-affected encounter at Bradford at the beginning of June, Yorkshire's 146, thanks mainly to Ephraim Lockwood's 66, gave them an 18-run first-innings lead and they were 30/3 chasing 118 to win when time ran out. Peate took eight Australian wickets. The Aussies were back in Yorkshire at Sheffield on 19 June. While Yorkshire were all out for 92, Peate took seven wickets for 51 when the tourists replied with 148. A battling 153 gave the Aussies a challenge, which they met with six wickets to spare. So the selectors must have taken good notice of the way the Australians found Peate difficult to face. Of their 33 wickets to fall in the two county matches, Peate had taken 17 of them. The *Yorkshire Post* commented: 'The Australians were nonplussed by the bowling of Bates and Peate, the wickets being just in that biting condition that suits Bates. It appears to matter little to Peate whether the wickets are soft or hard as he is successful no matter what condition the ground is in.'

Bates and Peate were deadly in tandem, helped by a cold, wet summer. An innings win over Kent and ten-wicket victory over Sussex seemed to put an end to the talk of bringing in the amateurs. The win against Kent was a milestone for Peate – a first hat-trick. The *Yorkshire Post* did not exactly enthuse over this. It limited its comment to 'Peate secured three wickets with his last three balls, thus performing the hat-trick.' His three victims were Lord Harris, Lord Throwley and Edward O'Shaugnessy. Still, it fitted a contemporary joke that Peate told saying he 'knocked over the House of Lords and Home Rule in three balls' with Harris and Throwley representing the House of Lords and Irishman O'Shaugnessy Home Rule. At the time, the question of Home Rule for Ireland (a sort of early devolution which has today produced separate parliaments for Scotland and Wales) was the premier political issue of the day and Peate's quip would have been widely understood. Today it falls flat but it does shed a little light on Peate's like of a good story. Peate went on to tell Pullin: 'For this hat-trick I was presented with a silver mount for a walking stick. Here it is. You will see it is in the form of a fist clasping a revolver. I now tell my friends it is a facsimile of a mailed fist, presented to me by the German emperor.' Peate evidently showed the silver mount to his interviewer but alas this memento of his feat, like so many relics of his life, has disappeared.

One final postscript – *Wisden* produced a book which is an anthology of its writings on Yorkshire and at the end an appendix listed records, such as leading run-makers, highest scores, etc. Among them is a list of hat-tricks. There's Allen Hill's against Surrey in 1880 and George Ulyett's against Lancashire but no mention of Ted Peate's against Kent in 1882, nor of one he was to achieve a couple of years later against Gloucestershire.

Another easy win over a strong Nottinghamshire team followed before Yorkshire faced the Australians three times in a row in ten days in matches at Dewsbury, Bradford and Middlesbrough starting on 13 July and ending on 22 July. The Yorkshire fixtures attracted big crowds – 15,000 at Bradford – and boosted the coffers of the tourists, who were on a share of the gate. The matches were perhaps most notable for the appearance of the Honourable Martin Hawke. While individual players did shine in some of the games, there was not a combined performance to defeat the all-conquering tourists. The Dewsbury match was ended by rain inconclusively but Australia won the other two.

Another notable match was at Old Trafford on 3–5 August when Peate found himself in the unusual position of not only top scoring in the Yorkshire first innings but opening the batting in their second. Peate's 38 rescued Yorkshire, who were 83/7 when he came in but rallied to 158 all out. There were only seven minutes of play left when Lancashire's second innings was wrapped up, setting Yorkshire a target of matching their first innings score of 158 to win. Peate nicked a single from the first over's last ball to retain the strike and in the second over hit a boundary and a three to walk off with an unbeaten 8 to his name and doubtless some ribald comments from Emmett, who had watched it from the non-striker's end. The fun continued the following day as Peate advanced to 21 before falling. Apart from Emmett, Yorkshire again struggled and were all out 15 short of victory. Lancashire went on to be adjudged the co-county champions with Nottinghamshire.

Peate lined up against the Australians for the sixth time that summer as he was in the Players' team to face them at The Oval on 11 August. There were reported to be huge crowds to see the finest professionals in the land, which included Yorkshire's famous four – Ulyett, Lockwood, Bates and Peate. The Australians had waltzed through their fixtures but to the delight of the crowd, Maurice Read, on his own ground, scored 130 and, backed up by 80 from

Nottinghamshire's Billy Barnes, the Players advanced to 322. Peate opened the bowling for the Players and had Charles Bannerman out for a duck (Bannerman is famous in Test history for his 'hat-trick' of achievements – facing the first ever ball in Test cricket, scoring the first run and the first century). The Australians were skittled out for 150 and then 138 (five wickets in total for Peate) to provide a convincing victory for the Players.

Yorkshire's hopes of finishing as recognised champions were to end at Cheltenham, heavily beaten by Gloucestershire. In their end of season review published on 28 August, the *Yorkshire Post* reflected on an ultimately disappointing season. After the four tourists had performed so well in Australia in the winter, the opening fixture against Nottinghamshire had seen an ignominious defeat. Another reverse at Middlesex had 'caused a lot of grumbling' and calls for fresh men to be brought in. Considering the *Yorkshire Post* itself had been one of those making the call, it had a bit of a cheek to warn: 'There are always a lot of egotists who have panaceas for all evils … There has already in former years been too much chopping in the Yorkshire team.' The newspaper revealed one good reason why Yorkshire preferred to stick to professionals when it noted 'the many disappointments they previously had by amateurs failing to keep their appointments at the last moment'.

There were two notable debuts for Yorkshire in the 1882 season. Peate suffered a sprained ankle and was unable to play against Surrey in June. His replacement was Bobby Peel, who was only two years younger and would go on to replace him long-term in the team. Another was Lord Hawke, who made his county championship debut in the same game. It was a dramatic finish as Yorkshire were left with just half an hour to score 44 runs in their second innings for victory but fell nine runs short. The *Post* put the blame on Hawke for scoring his 10 too slowly. Hawke would go on to play eight matches, scoring 212 runs at an average of 14.2. Peel too was not discarded, playing six matches, taking 23 wickets for 329 runs at an average of 14.7. The weekly magazine *Cricket* marked Peel out as a promising player but who was too much like Peate to dislodge him from the team.

At home, Yorkshire were undefeated by any county, beating Derbyshire, Kent, Sussex, Nottinghamshire, Gloucestershire and Middlesex and having the better of rain-affected draws against Lancashire and Surrey. Their eight away matches saw them beat Surrey, Derbyshire and Sussex but lose to Nottinghamshire, Middlesex, Lancashire, Gloucestershire and Kent. Peate dominated the bowling averages (which officially included only performances against other county sides), taking more than twice as many wickets as his nearest challenger (Billy Bates). In his 15 matches Peate bowled 1,010 overs, 475 of them maidens, and took 116 wickets for 1,212 runs, an average of 10.52. The *Yorkshire Post* clung to its conviction that Peate would make a good batsman, pointing out that he had again top scored for his team in the second innings of their final match against Kent. The author got a bit carried away when he said, 'In time Peate may earn the eminent distinction achieved this year by Barlow of being not only the premier batsman but also the first bowler for his county.' The Barlow referred to is Dick Barlow of Lancashire.

Chapter 6

Peak Peate

TED PEATE gave very few interviews during his lifetime. The modern Test cricketer has a microphone shoved up his nose at every opportunity, their everyday life is pored over in magazines and newspapers, they are encouraged to give their thoughts on social media in the hope that it might lead to a lucrative media career once retirement beckons. It was not like that in the Victorian era. The media was much smaller, limited to newspapers and magazines which rarely strayed outside of straight reportage of a cricket match and whose audience would only see the unfolding of a match if they were physically at the ground and had their eyes on the action. The result is that Peate's character is tantalisingly elusive. He left little trail for posterity to follow. He kept no diary, there are no surviving letters and his personal mementoes have vanished, quite possibly thrown out as unwanted clutter. Like footsteps on a light snowfall, traces of Ted vanished quickly. We are therefore left to piece together the surviving evidence to try to get a grip on the man who posterity has labelled as dissolute, difficult and a dipsomaniac.

One thing that becomes apparent is that Peate was part of a quartet of senior players who were determined to have a good time both on and off the field. This is not to say that they were careless about winning. However, their working-class roots impressed upon them the fact that their cricketing talent was time-limited, that when their career was over there was no family wealth to sustain their standard of living. The other three members of this band were Tom Emmett, George Ulyett and Ephraim Lockwood.

Emmett was the ringleader as well as being Yorkshire captain. He was renowned for his easy-going character and wisecracking. Anecdotes of his sayings are legion, the sort that would stuff many an after-dinner cricket speech today. Emmett would himself be delighted to have been on the sporting dinner circuit had it existed and his interview with Alfred Pullin is full of tales of his mischievous attitude to the game. Jim Carr's *Dictionary of Extra-Ordinary Cricketers* relates how he 'politely asked of an Australian fielder who had crept in close if he was wed. He explained that although he had no compunction about killing him, the death of a husband and father would vex his peace of mind.' *Wisden's* obituary was generous in its summation: 'The charm of Emmett as a cricketer lay in his keen and obvious enjoyment of the game. No day was too long for him and up to the end he played with the eagerness of a schoolboy. He was full of humour and numberless good stories are told about him.' Indeed they are, although most have been decanted through time and their origin is mysterious, not to say dubious.

Emmett's career with Yorkshire lasted from 1866 to 1887, the year after Peate's own career was terminated, but ended with some bitterness. His obituary in *Wisden* stated: 'His closing days were unhappily rather clouded but on this point there is no need to dwell.' Emmett himself was less reticent in describing his last days, telling Pullin: 'When I did finish a remark was made by someone in authority which hurt me very much. I asked if I should be wanted and the reply was "No, we don't want to see you any more." It may have been meant as a joke but it was not well put; after my long service to the county it seemed in bad taste and I felt it.'

Ulyett was quieter but no less fun-loving than Emmett. He was known as Happy Jack and was reputed to have ended one match in club cricket with two black eyes, one from a sharply rising ball and the other from fighting with an opponent. When touring America with Emmett he found out that his colleague was terrified of snakes. Ulyett found a piece of rubber tubing and shoved it in Emmett's sock while he was batting and then warned his fellow Yorkshireman that he had seen a snake slithering around his clothing. Lord Hawke related in his autobiography how Ulyett, while playing for England, was invited round to the home of the wealthy Studds for breakfast. (This must have been the famous 'Ashes' Test of 1882 as Studd did not play again for England after February 1883.) A jug of Devonshire cream was mistakenly put on the table. Ulyett, who was eating lamb chops at the time, looked at it quizzically and then poured the jug's contents over his chops and ate the lot. Hawke had a soft spot for Ulyett, whose career with Yorkshire lasted from 1873 to 1893, and said of him: 'It has always been my impression that if he had taken his cricket a little more seriously he might have been yet more valuable. To him every match was simply a jolly game and he did not care if he made a duck or a century.'

The third member of the trio was the quietest. Ephraim Lockwood had a dry sense of humour and he tagged along with Emmett, Ulyett and, later, Peate. There is a photograph of the four taken in a Cambridge photographic studio in which they put on gowns and mortar boards to pose as graduates of the university reading books. Both Hawke and Emmett tell the story of how, on a tour of America, the English cricketers were taken to Niagara Falls and Lockwood was distinctly unimpressed. In a comment which would endear him to all true Yorkshiremen, he said he would rather be back home in Huddersfield which was just as pretty. Pullin found Lockwood a difficult person to interview. Their conversation opened with Lockwood stating he had 'Nowt to say' about his career. Most books say his nickname was 'Mary Ann', but Lockwood himself says it was 'Old Mary'. He told Pullin: 'I owe my name of "Old Mary" to George Freeman … I was fielding at long slip to Freeman's bowling and as the ball shot towards me George shouted out "Look alive, Old Mary." I became Old Mary from that day.'

All three were well-established in the Yorkshire side when Peate burst on to the scene. He soon gravitated towards them, and they relished the pranks they played on each other. On one occasion Peate and Lockwood were playing in the Gentlemen v Players match at The Oval. As they were ready to go to the ground Peate left his watch on the dressing room table at the hotel and left the room door open. Lockwood, passing by, spotted the watch, sneaked in and put it in his pocket – for safety he would later say. Later Peate discovered the loss at the ground and thought someone had stolen the watch from the dressing room. He complained bitterly about the theft and earned the sympathy of W.G. Grace and Lord Harris, who advised him to report the matter to the police. 'We roused all Scotland Yard up nearly and I was busy for about a fortnight making inquiries about my missing watch,' Peate told Pullin. 'At last, when I thought I had seen the last of it, Ephraim quietly handed it over to me as if nothing had happened. He and the others had had a fortnight's quiet chuckling at my expense.' The story is typical of the practical jokes the quartet got up to. This time the police launched an investigation and the jokers realised they could not come clean until things had calmed a little.

Another of their larks concerned Ulyett and Peate after a match at The Oval. The hot political topic of the early

1880s was Home Rule for Ireland with William Gladstone's Liberal government attempting to bring in a measure of devolved government for the country. It was accompanied by a campaign of bombing by extremist Irish nationalists which had seen dynamite explosions at various places in the capital including Scotland Yard, Victoria station and Whitehall. Ulyett and Peate had decided to have a look at the Prime Minister's official residence (this was in the days before security controls made Downing Street out of bounds to the general public). They saw how numerous carriages were arriving and found out that Gladstone was holding an official reception for the Queen's birthday. The two Yorkshiremen decided they too would like to attend. Ulyett walked straight past the officials pretending to be deaf and Peate followed saying, 'My friend is deaf and I must follow him.' Their bravado worked and they got into the official reception where they were spotted by a famous Lancashire cricketer (presumably an amateur of considerable means) who challenged them. Ulyett's reply, as told by Peate to Pullin, was 'Oh, we thought it was a place of entertainment so we thought we would just look in.' The pair stayed a while, had a drink, and then walked leisurely out. Peate expressed his surprise that in the middle of a terrorist campaign against the government they had been able to walk past police and straight into 10 Downing Street.

Charlie Ullathorne, a bit part player with Yorkshire, told a story that he went with Ulyett and Peate for dinner while staying at the Crown Court Hotel for a match against Surrey and ordered steak for three. 'In due course it came – a big porterhouse steak in a dish. The waiter placed it opposite Ulyett, who promptly helped himself to the lot. We sat expectant for a few minutes and then called the waiter and asked when our share was likely to make its appearance. "Beg pardon gentlemen, but you ordered steak for three and I brought it." "What?" said Ulyett. "This for three! Nonsense; bring the gentlemen one apiece. We always grow them this size in our county."' Typical Yorkshire – the biggest and best!

When Ulyett died in 1898 *Cricket* magazine published his obituary in their 23 June edition. It included another anecdote about the playful characters of the Yorkshire side. According to them a young cricketer in his debut season turned up at a Yorkshire ground (the article is unspecific on names and places) and, because the wicket was wet, he wanted to get in some practice before taking on Peate. The debutant opened the batting for his county and had been piling up the runs. Just at that moment two men in civvies turned up and the new boy asked them if they would bowl a few at him in the nets so he could get his eye in. The two men said they played a bit of club cricket but were nowhere near good enough to play for Yorkshire and were just there to watch the game and pick up a few tips from Ulyett and Peate. Of course, the two 'spectators' were the real Ulyett and Peate and both sent down deliveries which the youngster found unplayable, so much that he was unnerved. If two mere spectators could bamboozle him, what must Ulyett and Peate be like? His side opened the batting and the inexperienced lad walked out to the wicket to find the two 'spectators' grinning widely at him.

These stories give a flavour of Peate's assimilation into the very heart of the Yorkshire dressing room. He was not a ringleader but he was a willing participant in the light-hearted antics. However, there was a ruthless streak in Peate. Another story told by Pullin concerns again a Gentlemen v Players match. Peate was batting and he stepped back for a pull shot which he sent to the boundary for four. Looking down he spotted that he had brushed the leg stump and dislodged the bail so he moved into a position where neither umpire could quite see the leg stump. The wicketkeeper appealed but the umpire turned it down. The wicketkeeper urged Peate to do the right thing and return to the pavilion but Peate stood his ground, replaced the bail and continued with his innings.

He was also capable of kindness and remained in touch with his humble origins. The *Yorkshire Post* of 8 February 1886 noted that 'Mr E Peate, the famous Yorkshire bowler, distributed soup to over 100 poor families in Yeadon on Friday and Saturday. It is said that the distress in the village, resulting from the storm, is such that there is plenty of scope for the exercise of such commendable generosity as that which Mr Peate is showing.' This was not the only occasion on which he supported a good cause. In September 1883 Peate played without payment for Hodgson and Simpson, a Wakefield team supported by a soap factory, in a benefit match against Halifax. The club's professional, Samuel Dennison, had died of typhus during the summer, leaving a widow and six children. There were other instances of turning out for charity. In 1893 the *Craven Herald* reported that Peate had donated half his match fee playing for Skipton to a fund set up to support the family of a member of the Skipton rugby club, who played on the adjacent field. He had died from a rugby injury, but the Yorkshire Rugby Football Union refused to countenance a contribution from the rugby club as it would break their 'amateur' ethos. The *Craven Herald* is also the source of one of the few comments on his character but it fits in with the happy, light-hearted image suggested by his membership of the four pranksters: 'Whether it was during a lull in the game or an after-dinner speech at the Ship Hotel, he was equally happy and sure of an admiring and responsive argument.'

Peate started the 1883 season with the accolade of a front-page profile in the weekly *Cricket* magazine on Thursday, 31 May. He already held the record of most wickets taken in a season for Yorkshire (156) and was widely recognised as the best spin bowler in the country in the days when spin was at least as popular in a bowling attack as seam or pace. Six years earlier he had been a 'clown' cricketer. Now, at the age of 27, he was feared throughout the land. The article in *Cricket* points out his rapid rise: 'To attain the very topmost rung of the ladder within a period of four years is a feat which has fallen to the lot of few, very few, professional cricketers. Yet this enviable distinction can fairly be claimed by the young player whose portrait we give this week, Edmund Peate ... It is safe to say that no slow bowler has ever achieved such a record in the first year of his appearance and, in proof of his success, reference need only be made to his figures in 1879 for Yorkshire, which showed 675 overs, 258 maidens, 752 runs and 65 wickets.' (Note – these figures are slightly different from the ones proffered by the *Yorkshire Post*.) The magazine details his remarkable figures and says that he was the 'most successful trundler of the day' and it was no surprise that he was selected for first the Players v Gentlemen representative game and then invited to join Alfred Shaw's touring side to Australia.

It said his performances on the tour 'were of the most brilliant kind and the members of the colonial teams which had starred in England in 1878 and 1880 were unanimous in accounting him the best English bowler they had seen. Peate, Bates and Midwinter had to bear the brunt of the bowling of the team, but the left-hander was infinitely the most successful of the trio and his analysis of that tour, 1,382 overs for 1,544 runs and 264 wickets for an average of 5.85 per wicket was in every way an extraordinary achievement. During a portion of the last season of 1882 he was suffering from the great disadvantage of a sprained ankle and this made his brilliant successes the more surprising.'

The article ends with a critique of his style: 'Peate is, beyond a doubt, the best slow bowler of the present day.

His delivery (left hand) is very easy, his accuracy of pitch is unerring. He varies his bowling too with great judgement. He generally works away from the off but occasionally bowls a most difficult ball coming with his arm. He alters the pace and height of the ball too, cleverly, and when he finds a spot to help him the best batsmen find it impossible to score. As a batsman he has more than once proved useful at the finish of an innings and has frequently been of great service to the Yorkshire eleven at a crisis. Some of his batting, during the tour of Shaw's team in Australia, was very creditable and he has several times surprised the spectators by the resistance he has offered to the best bowlers. Fielding is, perhaps, his worst point but even in this department he is not a failure. There are few better-conducted cricketers than Edmund Peate and it need hardly be added that his general popularity is thoroughly well deserved.'

He started 1883 with a lucrative appearance for a team funded by Wakefield soap manufacturers Hodgson and Simpson who played Hull Town on Saturday, 12 May (this was the same team for whom, when the county season was over, Peate was to return to, unpaid, for the charity match in aid of the widow and six children of its late professional). On the Monday after this first appearance for the soap side, Peate was at Lord's for the North v South match. He was back to his frugal best and took 12-62 with only W.G. Grace providing much resistance with 64 before becoming one of Peate's victims (and then absenting himself in the South's second innings with an injured hand). The first county match was against MCC at Lord's which Yorkshire won by ten wickets in two days, giving them the opportunity to head out to Epsom on the Wednesday to watch the Derby before taking on a Lord Hawke-led Cambridge University on the Thursday.

At Dewsbury on 7 June against Kent, Yorkshire won by an innings using only Peate and their new fast bowler George

Ted Peate studio portrait taken at the height of his fame

The Yorkshire team which played Sussex at Brighton in August 1884: Back row: Ted Peate, Tom Emmett, Mr Turner (scorer), William Harris, Joe Hunter. Middle: John Rawlin, Fred Lee, Louis Hall, Bobby Peel, George Ulyett. Front: Billy Bates, Irwin Grimshaw

Illustrated London News print depicting the final day of the 1882 Oval Test match

The honours board at Lord's with Ted's name heading the list. Picture courtesy of MCC/Jed Leicester

ENGLAND

Year	Player	Opponent	Figures		Year	Player
1884	E. Peate	Australia	6-85		1984	I.T. Botha[m]
	G. Ulyett	Australia	7-36			I.T. Botha[m]
1886	J. Briggs	Australia	11-74		1985	I.T. Botha[m]
1893	W.H. Lockwood	Australia	6-101		1988	G.R. Dille[y]
1896	J.T. Hearne	Australia	5-76		1990	D.E. Malc[olm]
	T. Richardson	Australia	11-173			A.R.C. Fr[aser]
1907	E.G. Arnold	South Africa	5-37		1991	D.R. Prin[gle]
1909	A.E. Relf	Australia	5-85			P.A.J. DeF[reitas]
1912	F.R. Foster	South Africa	5-16			P.C.R. Tuf[nell]
	S.F. Barnes	South Africa	11-110		1995	A.R.C. Fr[aser]
1931	I.A.R. Peebles	New Zealand	5-77			D.G. Cork
1933	R.W.V. Robins	West Indies	6-32		1998	D.G. Cork
1934	H. Verity	Australia	15-104		2000	E.S.H. Gi[ddins]
1936	G.O. Allen	India	10-78			

A postcard from 1885 depicting the best XI in England. Centre: W.G. Grace.
Clockwise from top: Hon A. Lyttleton, A. Shrewsbury, W. Bates, Mr W.W. Read, G.
Ulyett, R.G. Barlow, E. Peate, Mr A.G. Steele, W. Gunn, W. Barnes.
Courtesy of Neil Windle

*Ephraim
Lockwood, Ted
Peate, George
Ulyett and
Tom Emmett
in playful
mood wearing
the gowns of
Cambridge
graduates.*
Courtesy of
Neil Windle

*Lord Martin
Bladen Hawke,
Peate's nemesis*

Yorkshire in 1885, Peate's last full season. Back row, left to right: George Ulyett, Bobby Peel, William Woodhouse, Mr Turner (scorer), Joe Hunter. Seated: Billy Bates, Ted Peate, Louis Hall (captain), Tom Emmett, Fred Lee. Front: Joe Preston, Irwin Grimshaw.

The Yorkshire team in 1887, the year Peate was sacked. Back row left to right: Joe Hunter, Saul Wade, Joe Preston. Seated: Billy Bates, Louis Hall, Lord Martin Hawke, Tom Emmett, George Ulyett, Fred Lee. Front: Joe Denton, Bobby Peel. Peate, Woodhouse and Grimshaw have gone from the 1885 photograph, replaced by Wade, Hawke and Denton.

Yeadon Cricket Club, Ted's spiritual home

Skipton Cricket Club, where Ted was engaged as club professional from 1893 to 1899

Peate seated middle row fourth from right in white shirt on tour to Holland 1893
Picture courtesy of Neil Windle

Ted's sports shop in the Headrow (now occupied by AZ Nails and Tiger Sugar)

Ted's house in Granby View, Headingley, where he lived for most of the 1890s

Pencil drawing of Ted Peate used to illustrate Old Ebor's interview in the Yorkshire Evening Post in 1898

E. PEATE
(Up-to-date)

A cutting from Ted's local newspaper showing him a few weeks before his death with his faithful dog. Original copies of this photograph have been lost.

In 1893 The Graphic *newspaper carried this rather cruel drawing of Ted Peate to illustrate an article on the tour to Holland. It emphasised his physical decline by adding 'up to date' under his name.* Picture courtesy of Alan Shaw.

The site of Ted Peate's grave with no headstone in Yeadon Cemetery

Harrison, playing his first county match, in both innings. Peate took 9-79 and Harrison 10-56 (the other wicket was run out). However, Yorkshire's inconsistency was shown up again when they were surprisingly beaten by three runs by Sussex. Peate took only one wicket but top scored in the first innings with 29 and was run out for 30 in the second as Yorkshire desperately chased the victory. Such figures would have given heart to those who remained convinced that he could step up to being an all-rounder.

As well as his county fixtures, Peate was also open for guest appearances. On 16 June the Orleans Cricket Club must have paid a tidy sum to hire Yorkshire's four tourists to Australia – Peate, Bates, Ulyett and Emmett – and bring them down to London for a one-day game. Orleans were a well-connected club named after their ground at Orleans Road, Twickenham. Among their members was cricket fanatic Charles Inglis Thornton, who founded the Scarborough Cricket Festival. The club only survived ten years yet four of their games are considered to be first-class matches – including one against the Australian tourists in 1878. Peate and Ulyett were asked to play for Elsenham (a village club from Essex whose connection to the Orleans club is unknown although it was home to Sir Walter Gilbey, of Gilbey's Gin fame) while Bates and Emmett lined up for Orleans. All four were back in Yorkshire on the Monday for a Yorkshire and Nottinghamshire combined team to take on England at Bradford. The hectic nature of the professional is shown by the fact that this match was finished on the Wednesday and the following morning the same four were back in London walking out at The Oval for the North v South match. Whether they stayed overnight or caught an early train in the morning is not recorded.

On 28 June Peate was selected for the traditional Gentlemen and Players match at The Oval which resulted in a large crowd running on to the pitch at the end in excitement. Peate was heavily involved. In a close finish, the scores were tied with the Gentlemen having only one wicket remaining. Peate had failed to take a wicket in the entire match when he was thrown the ball and with his second delivery he bowled the unfortunate Hugh Rotherham to secure the tie and avoid defeat for the Players. 'There was great enthusiasm at the finish and it was some time before the excitement of the spectators had subsided,' said *Cricket* magazine.

At this time the *Yorkshire Post* ran an interesting correspondence about the team selection which had been sparked by that 'defeat to a third rate county [Sussex]' which it described as galling. The newspaper had criticised the Sheffield-based Yorkshire committee for ignoring new talent and allowing the established team to become complacent. It asked its readers to send in their suggestions for Yorkshire's best XI choosing from existing county players and rising amateurs and professionals. The paper then selected 50 of what it claimed was a very large number of replies. Of these 50, five players were selected by all correspondents – Ulyett, Hall, Bates, Lockwood and Peate. The long-serving captain Emmett, who was now on the far side of 40, was chosen by 39. The paper commented that the top five 'retain their well-earned position of champions of their county, an honour to which they are fully entitled by the great prowess shown in the feat of play'. In this test of public opinion, Peate was significantly ahead of the man who would eventually inherit his mantle, Bobby Peel, who was less than two years his junior. Peel was only selected by 15 of the correspondents. Of course, this is a very unscientific sample but it is some of the best evidence we have that the Peate and Bates pairing was considered unassailable and that Peate had the dominant role.

On 23 July Peate achieved the best bowling figures of his career when Yorkshire thrashed Surrey at Holbeck. Ironically, it followed a rather lean spell for him culminating in the Roses match three weeks previously when Lancashire had made their then record lowest innings score. Despite Lancashire scoring just 219 in both innings, Peate failed to take a wicket and was barely used in the second innings. The return fixture took place at Bramall Lane just ten days later and Peate was not even in the Yorkshire team – whether injured, unavailable or dropped is unclear. However, he was back for the Surrey game. The *Cricket* magazine report states: 'When Surrey went in they made a poor show and Peate did an extraordinary performance. In sixteen overs he took eight wickets at a cost of only five runs. He was, of course, helped very materially by the ground but none the less it was a wonderful feat and Peate's success is the more gratifying as this season he has been rather out of luck.' When Peate gave his interview to Alfred Pullin he gave an amusing postscript to his most successful day. Normally he might expect a collection to be made to reward his achievement but Holbeck had fought long and hard for a match on the county circuit. Peate's skills had turned a three-day match into a two-day affair with the attendant loss of gate money. When it was suggested that the traditional hat be passed round for contributions, an unidentified man, probably a member of the Holbeck committee, was furious: 'Oh be ---- [the blank was inserted in the original]. He has ruined our gate. I object to the hat going round.'

This was a scheduled three-day match from 23–25 July with, incredibly to a modern fan, the return fixture at The Oval due to start the next day, 26 July. As the Yorkshire side clinched their win inside two days, there was an extra day to travel down. However, Peate did not go with them. The *Yorkshire Post*, normally a staunch supporter of him, was acerbic in its criticism: 'Peate was again an absentee and many are now asking how it is that he is usually away when the wicket is in hard condition.'

He was back on 30 July when Gloucestershire were the visitors to Park Avenue, Bradford, but failed to take a wicket. At least he did offer further evidence of improvement as a batsman as he made 61 in a convincing Yorkshire victory. Significantly, the top scorer, with 74, was the young man who was emerging ever more strongly as his rival, Bobby Peel. While Peate was wicketless and only bowled 21 overs in the entire match, Peel bowled 38 with two wickets, although it was Tom Emmett and the rising fast bowler George Harrison who did the damage with eight apiece.

While 1883 was not as glorious as the previous year, it would be harsh to conclude that Peate was on the decline even if there was the constant accusation that he was only truly dangerous on a wet pitch. He had, after all, returned those figures of 8-5 which were to be supreme for decades to come. True, he was no longer bowling marathon. spells as the emergence of Bobby Peel and George Harrison gave Emmett more options (himself included) but he was still the dangerman for opponents, particularly if the weather had been wet. *Cricket* magazine printed two sets of averages. In county games Peate was second in the Yorkshire averages in a close-run battle with Harrison. Peate had bowled 561 overs, but Harrison had eight more. The number of maidens was similar – 258 for Peate, 247 for Harrison – but it was the new man who had struck more often and at a better average. Peate had 59 wickets at an average of 12.15 while Harrison had 81 at 11.42. *Cricket* magazine also compiled a list of country-wide averages which included 'county and first-class matches' – i.e. games such as Lancashire and Yorkshire Combined XI v England, the two Players v Gentlemen contests, Nottinghamshire and Yorkshire Combined XI v England,

Yorkshire v Ivo Bligh's team (that was the side which had just returned from a tour of Australia), Yorkshire v MCC and the Varsity matches. Using these matches Peate found himself relegated to the third-ranked Yorkshire bowler just behind Harrison and Emmett with Peel snapping at his heels. On this analysis (according to the *Cricket* edition of 25 October 1883) the figures were: Harrison 786 overs, 1,325 runs, 100 wickets, average 13.25; Emmett 495-785-56-14.02; Peate 1,376-1,753-120-14.61; Peel 519-806-51-15.80.

On these statistics Yorkshire had four of the best eight bowlers in the land – little wonder that some questioned why they were behind Nottinghamshire in the county rankings. Their new fast bowler, Harrison, was a shooting star who shone brightly but briefly across the sky. He was the first cricketer to take 100 first-class wickets in his debut season. Born in Scarborough, he left his job as a shoemaker to become a professional cricketer and in this his breakthrough season was deemed good enough to play for the Players against the Gentlemen. Like Peate, he had emerged through the colts trial match despite not being asked to bowl in the first innings. When he finally got hold of the ball he took 9-14, including six in seven balls with four in a row, a dot ball and then two more. Every one of these six wickets was clean bowled! His rapid ascent to gain inclusion in the Players team seemed not to go down too well with W.G. Grace, who instructed the Gentlemen to hit him out of the ground. Harrison was later quoted as saying, 'When I got back to the hotel I couldn't eat me dinner. I took off me boots and let me feet cool on the oilcloth. Then I got into bed and cried like a baby.' There was no real disgrace and although he conceded more than 100 runs, he did take three wickets. Yorkshire were not put off and he featured regularly in the team for the 1883 season. The *Yorkshire Post* described Harrison at the end of the 1883 season as 'probably the best fast bowler ever seen in Yorkshire, certainly the most deadly of his class in England at this present moment'.

Then, in the 1884 season, he dislocated his shoulder while acting as a replacement fielder for Gloucestershire. He was never able to bowl again at the fast pace he had in that remarkable first season. He took only 18 wickets in ten first-class matches in 1884 and drifted out of the team and into league cricket with Bradford sides Idle and Bowling Old Lane. He did make a comeback, with a different action, and in 1890 and 1891 he took 123 wickets in total but he was never the same threat. He lost his place to George Hirst, returned to Bowling Old Lane and then became a first-class umpire.

1883 was also a significant year in Peate's private life. His wife Sarah had given birth to their second child, a daughter who was christened Lizzie. Then he opened a sports shop at 8 Upperhead Row in the centre of Leeds selling cricket equipment. He had the example of team-mate Ephraim Lockwood to follow. Lockwood had opened a similar shop in his hometown of Huddersfield and the two ran adverts side by side on a weekly basis in the *Yorkshire Post*. Peate showed sound business sense with a publicity coup to mark the opening of his shop. The Yorkshire Challenge Cup had been started five years earlier and was contested by the leading football (which at that time meant rugby) clubs in the county. Despite misgivings from the game's governing body, this first ever rugby knockout trophy proved a huge success, drawing large crowds and the subsequent financial rewards. It was dominated by the clubs who, a decade later, would finally lose patience with the snobbery and discrimination of the southern-dominated rugby hierarchy at Twickenham and form the rival code of rugby league in an argument over compensating players who lost wages to play for their club. Peate was savvy enough to arrange for the cup to be displayed in his shop window, thus guaranteeing large crowds who would come to view the first ever rugby knockout trophy. In the days leading up to the 23 April final between Wakefield Trinity and Halifax at Cardigan Fields in Headingley, the cup could be seen in the front window of Peate's new shop. Spectators could get a close-up view of the trophy which was causing such excitement for the many followers of the premier winter sport.

Peate was to keep the shop going until his death and it may explain why he never toured Australia again. In the winter of 1883/84 Ivo Bligh took a team consisting of eight amateurs and four professionals out to Australia and while it is unknown if Peate was invited and turned it down, his rival in the Yorkshire team, Billy Bates, was in the touring party. With the need to establish the shop, and a young baby just arrived, there was no possibility of a lengthy trip overseas and nor was there a chance that Peate would be back in the mills. Instead he was to build up the shop which was to keep him ticking over in winter. It was not easy. While he and Lockwood were the only ones advertising in the *Yorkshire Post* in 1883, they were soon joined by rivals, two of them close to Peate in the centre of Leeds. The 1884 newspapers carry advertisements by W Duthoit Cricketers Outfitters on Boar Lane and Croisdale Cricketers Outfitters on Briggate.

Peate had the advantage of his famous name but he showed some business acumen by expanding the range of goods. Tennis and (rugby) football goods were added by 1884 and *Kelly's Leeds Directory* of 1888 describes his shop as a 'sports outfitter and tobacconist'. The advertisements also reflect the changing market. By 1887 he was calling the shop 'the Yorkshire County Football and Athletic Warehouse' and had added parlour games, compendiums, draughts, chess, dominoes, cards and 'winter games' to his advert. By 1895 he had also added lacrosse, croquet and bowls to the stock although the indoor games seem to have disappeared. Football now also meant Association as well as the rugby version. He was also not afraid to make grandiose claims about the shop. Had there been a Victorian equivalent to the Advertising Standards Authority they would surely have taken issue with the boast that it was the 'largest and best selected stock in the kingdom'. It is difficult to assess just how lucrative the shop proved to be. When he died he was financially just keeping his head above water but his widow could not afford to pay for his funeral. Whether that was because Peate was not a good businessman and the shop barely turned a profit or because the profits were poured into an attempt to maintain a lifestyle which his income did not warrant is unclear.

The building where Peate's shop stood still exists, one of the few buildings to survive largely intact on the street, a couple of hundred yards from Leeds Town Hall. Upperhead Row is now called simply The Headrow and the shop, back then number 8, has been subdivided into two shops, at the time of writing one being a nail bar, the other being an outlet selling Chinese 'bubble' tea. Backing on to the famous Leeds Variety Theatre, which in Peate's day would have been doing a roaring trade with music hall turns, the site, then and now called Thornton's Buildings, also contained a public house, the Horse and Trumpet, which is still serving beer to this day. Peate's shop was on the ground floor, the upper floors being devoted to offices, the largest being occupied by the *Magnet*, a weekly publication which described itself as 'a journal devoted to the interests of the music hall profession'. It provided news, gossip and information on a myriad of acts, forthcoming attractions and most importantly advertisements for everything to do with the industry: boarding houses for turns to stay in; vacancies for jugglers, acrobats, strong men, dancers, etc. and acts advertising their speciality and availability in breathless prose. Ironically, a regular advertisement was for a troupe of clown cricketers and performing dogs called The Brothers Pannoll. The *Magnet*'s proprietors appear to have been agents for this company as all enquiries are directed to them at Thornton's Buildings. Who knows if they discussed with Peate his clown cricketing past?

* * *

With the shop up and running, Peate was early into action on the cricket field in 1884, turning out for Woodhouse Temperance CC (the irony of a supposedly renowned boozer like Peate playing for a team committed to teetotalism will not be lost on readers) on 12 April against Leeds Leamington. In the lead-up to the new season, Peate was widely rumoured to be considering a move to the United States to play in Philadelphia. A brief report in *Cricket* magazine of 31 January 1884 quotes a Sydney newspaper: 'The Merion club of Philadelphia is using every endeavour to secure the services of a good English professional and has offered £500 for the services of any one of the following professionals for next season: A Shaw, Bates, Barlow and Peate.' If the offer was real and reached Peate, he evidently declined but some contact must have been made for *Cricket* magazine later reported that he had been lined up to provide coaching sessions for a Philadelphian touring team which was due to arrive in England in May. Peate was also engaged to turn out again for Hodgson & Simpson's, who had emerged as one of the top club sides in Yorkshire. Their fixture list of more than 40 matches included contests against fellow powerhouses Lascelles Hall, Yorkshire Gentlemen, Hull and Manningham and they had John Thewlis junior, who had three appearances for Yorkshire under his belt and was the cousin of Ephraim

Lockwood, signed on as their regular professional. Their agreement with Peate was for him to play for them 'when not engaged to play in big matches'.

Despite his reputation as the best bowler in the land, there was widespread talk as the season began that Peate's place was under threat. *Cricket* magazine on 8 May said, 'Several rumours have been afloat this spring with regard to the composition of the Yorkshire eleven for this year and it is said that Emmett no longer retains the captaincy. Report has it that Hall will have charge of the eleven until the Hon. M.B. Hawke takes command; and it is also stated that Peate is not one of those who have received a regular retainer. Emmett, we have heard, will join the ground staff at Lord's and it is certainly difficult to see how he can even now be left out of any county eleven. At the same time, there appears to be no lack of good youngsters in Yorkshire and the principle of encouraging young talent is undoubtedly the right policy.' The report was correct in its forecast for the Yorkshire captaincy but Emmett still had three more effective seasons left in the side. He was now 43 and perhaps it was understandable that Hawke and the committee were looking to the future but Peate was still in his twenties and the rumour that Yorkshire were considering replacing him was met with widespread incredulity.

Yorkshire's season opened with a fixture against Gloucestershire and what a strong side Yorkshire put out, including Peate and Emmett. Hawke was now established as the captain – when available – and the other eight were Billy Bates, Louis Hall, George Harrison, Joseph Hunter, Ephraim Lockwood, Bobby Peel, Frank Sugg and George Ulyett. Of these, all but Harrison and Hall were or would go on to be England players – and Harrison and Hall had an outstanding record. Hopes must have been high that at last this Yorkshire team would fulfil their potential as they recorded a 41-run win away to W.G. Grace-led Gloucestershire. In the second innings Peate recorded spectacular figures of 18-10-13-6, including a hat-trick, his second for the county. His victims were W.G.'s brother Edward, John Painter and Charlie Townsend – Edward Grace and Townsend both played Test cricket. Peate later told the story of how the two teams were treated to a banquet at the home of an unnamed aristocrat after play on the second day. Yorkshire were only 29 runs ahead with six wickets remaining and things looked bleak. When W.G. Grace in his speech hinted at Gloucestershire's imminent victory Emmett, according to Peate, retorted: 'No, Doctor; we are Yorkshiremen and we have never lost until the last run is got or wicket taken.' The following day Peate scored 29 runs as Yorkshire set a target of 85 to win. Peate then got to work and secured a Yorkshire victory by 41 runs. He was presented with the match ball mounted on a plinth with an inscribed silver plate commemorating the hat-trick.

The *Yorkshire Post*'s comments on the match hint that behind the scenes, Peate was facing scrutiny. It said that his hugely impressive figures were 'surely sufficient evidence to show that the champion slow trundler has lost none of his form as those in authority at Sheffield have endeavoured of late to make us believe. No, he has proved the fears of even a slight decadence to be altogether groundless and now we hope to hear of his being again permanently reinstated in the team.' The choice of the word decadence is intriguing although not conclusive. It may have been used in its strictly literal meaning of decay, that his form was diminishing, rather than the wider meaning of low moral standards or behaviour. Either way, despite his outstanding county career to date, the *Yorkshire Post*'s comments confirm that questions were already being asked about his future. Plenty of food for thought for the new captain.

The newspaper was not the only one to criticise the committee for considering axing Peate. A letter was published which read: 'Why do not the committee of the Yorkshire County Eleven acknowledge publicly their sorrow in shelving the Grand Old Tom and Peate? I think it is due to the committee to at once make known their error as I am sure they cannot but confess that Peate as well as the Grand Old Tom have "G.O.T." as many wickets and made as many runs as the committee need desire. My name is a true one, viz Everybody's Opinion.' *Cricket* magazine, praising Peate's performance against Gloucestershire, said it could not consider any Yorkshire team which did not include Peate.

Whether or not the threat to Emmett and Peate was real, the Gloucestershire victory meant that both were, for now, undroppable. Peate starred against the Australian tourists in a low-scoring match at Bradford. Although Yorkshire lost by three wickets, his match figures were 10-62. The North of England also had few doubts about Peate's form as they selected him to play against his old foes the Australians at Old Trafford at the end of June and were rewarded with ten wickets as the Australians were beaten by an innings. The *Yorkshire Post* again were able to remark on the folly of the county selectors. While highlighting the performance of Lancashire batsmen Hornby and Barnes it said 'these performances, in the eyes of Yorkshiremen, pale before the remarkable form shown by their favourite bowler, Peate, who was undoubtedly the main cause of the decisive success. The Leeds man trundled unchanged throughout the two innings and in all captured ten wickets at a cost of 51 runs only – a very fine analysis on a hard, good wicket. He has on many occasions performed noteworthy feats but we doubt very much whether his latest wonderful figures have ever been reached under similar conditions. Yet this is the man the county committee had their doubts about the other week – the finest slow bowler in England at the present moment and without whom no team of an international character can be considered representative.' When Yorkshire played Lancashire, Lord Hawke presented Peate with the match ball from the North v Australia game 'mounted in gold' with the match result and Peate's performance inscribed. If Hawke really was thinking the unthinkable and getting rid of Peate he surely realised that his position was not strong enough and he would have to wait.

A third match against the Australians, who must by now have been entirely familiar with his strengths and weaknesses, followed at the beginning of July when Peate was selected for the Players XI. This match, at Bramall Lane, was marred when three of the professionals selected refused the £10 fee offered by the Yorkshire committee. They were the Nottinghamshire trio of Arthur Shrewsbury, Billy Barnes and Wilfred Flowers. The three were veterans of the Nottinghamshire Players' Strike of 1881 when they and four others refused to play for the county unless their pay was improved. Although they subsequently apologised and returned to the fold, they had laid down a marker. In their absence the Players were well beaten by six wickets (Peate taking all four Australian second-innings wickets).

The 1884 tour was the first time three matches against England were scheduled in this country and the first took place at Old Trafford on 10 July. Rain meant there was no play on the first day. England batted first and were all out for 95, although Shrewsbury showed his refusal to play for the Players a week earlier had not been permanently damaging to his England career by top scoring with 43. Peate bore the brunt of the bowling as Australia replied with 182. He bowled 49 overs taking 3-62 but the match fizzled out with England 182/9 in the second innings.

The second Test, the first ever to be staged on the Lord's ground, took place nine days later and it was here that Peate secured the prestige of becoming the first name on the famous honours board. Again, he bowled far more than any other player and again the Australians found him hard to score from but easy to get out to. He took 6-85 in 40 overs as the Australians reached 229 and it is this feat which is immortalised at the very top of the board at the home of English cricket. England responded with 379. In the second innings Peate went wicketless but his Yorkshire colleague George Ulyett followed him on to the board with an even more impressive 7-36. England had won by an innings and five runs. The third Test, at The Oval from 11 August, was a drawn affair, remarkable mainly for the fact that England used all 11 players as bowlers in the Australian first innings. Australia were 532/6 when W.G. Grace asked wicketkeeper Alfred Lyttleton to bowl. He took the last four Australian wickets, reputedly all with lobs. When the game ended the scores were Australia 551, England 346 and 85/2 (following on).

There was one match of particular note in the period between the second and third Test, and it took place at Sheffield when the Yorkshire Gentlemen took on the Yorkshire Players, resulting in a crushing win for the latter thanks mainly to Peate. He took 13 wickets, including Lord Hawke's in the second innings. This must have given Peate some satisfaction if he really was kicking back against the regime Lord Hawke was seeking to impose.

Peate was again involved in a controversial match against the Australians at The Oval when the Players took on the tourists. It was Peate's sixth appearance against the Australians that season but the match got off to a bad start when Nottinghamshire refused to release any of their players. In addition, Lancashire insisted that Richard

Barlow should play for them in a relatively unimportant match against the minor counties side Cheshire rather than for the Players. Therefore it was a much weakened Players team which turned up. There were six Yorkshiremen in the team – Peate, Ulyett, Hall, Bates, Emmett and the wicketkeeper Joseph Hunter (who despite being an England Test player was overshadowed by his brother, David, who succeeded him as Yorkshire's man behind the stumps). The crowd were already unhappy that some of the best players were unavailable and when the game began they were increasingly agitated. The Players, batting first, made 107, and the Australians replied with 151. Peate at least did his bit and again proved he was the one the tourists feared by taking 5-55. This included his 100th first-class wicket of the season and his 850th in total.

Play began on the second day of the scheduled three with the Players 5/1. It quickly became apparent that those who had paid their entrance fee were not going to see a full day's play as Fred Spofforth began to run riot. Only Ulyett, with 33, and Peate himself with 19 showed any resistance as Spofforth took 6/34 and the Players were all out for 71, leaving Australia with just a meagre 28 to win. They came out just before lunch and scored 17 in the first 15 minutes but, right on the stroke of lunch at two o'clock, Peate bowled George Bonnor. Although only 11 more were required, the Australians declined the invitation to carry on and finish the match and trooped off the field for their sandwiches. The Players remained on the pitch and waited while Tom Emmett, who was captain of the Players, followed the Australians to see if they wanted to finish the game, which could have been wrapped up inside ten minutes. However, the Australians decided to stand fast and stick to the 2pm lunch schedule. The crowd took it badly, started booing and a large number ran on to the pitch, pulling up the stumps.

Cricket magazine reported: 'For some time a certain section of the crowd remained in front of the pavilion behaving in a very disorderly manner. When the bell rang for a renewal at half past two, their attitude became still more hostile and the middle of the ground was not only occupied but the stumps sent flying. At last, after the arrival of a reinforcement of police and on Murdoch and McDonnell proceeding to the wickets, the crowd gradually cleared away from the centre and the game resumed at half past three.' During this hour's disruption, Peate was asked by Charles Alcock, the Surrey secretary and the same man who had organised the 1882 Ashes match, to speak to the crowd and persuade them to leave the pitch so the game could be concluded. Peate refused, later explaining: 'That was nothing in my line, so I told him "No thank you. I came here to play cricket, not to quell a riot."'

The *London Evening News* deplored the actions of the crowd and the necessity for a large detachment of police to clear the pitch. It said that while a verbal protest might have been understandable and no harm done, 'there was no justification for the people taking the course of action they did and turning the cricket field into a scene of riot'. The *Evening News* correspondent interviewed Australian captain Billy Murdoch to seek an explanation for insisting on lunch. The Australian must have had his tongue firmly in his cheek when he said the wicket was improving and he did not want his team to risk losing nine wickets and thus the match so he decided to allow it time to improve a little further.

The Aussies had not seen the back of Peate. Another match against the North of England at Nottingham from 1 September saw Peate turn out against them for the eighth time in a little over four months. It was a strong win for the North although Peate took only one wicket in the first innings and did not bowl at all in the second. The Australian captain and premier batsman Billy Murdoch was in no doubt about Peate's ability. He played 16 Tests for Australia against England between 1880 and 1890 and in an interview in *Cricket* magazine he rated Peate as the finest bowler he ever faced. Another Australian batsman, George Giffen, was to relate a story about Murdoch's difficulties with Peate which is quoted in Alfred Pullin's series of interviews. After one innings, in which he was beaten by a leg break, 'the batsman determined that it should not happen again, got hold of a bat in his room at the hotel and began to make strokes at imaginary balls. He would play back and mutter "That's the way to play you, Peate." Then he would play forward, remarking "Not this time, Peate, my boy." At last he ventured on a big hit at a leg ball and swinging round with a "How do you like that, Peate?" sent the toilet set, which he had forgotten about, in fragments on the floor. Later on in the day, confident he would make a score, he faced the real Peate and was clean bowled the first ball!'

Although Giffen did not name the batsman who smashed the toilet to pieces, Peate confirmed it was Murdoch and said he had been told this by Australian fast bowler Charlie Turner: 'Certainly I used to get his wicket very often. When he was over with the 1882 team I got his wicket oftener than any other bowler. There was one extraordinary innings he played too at Huddersfield in July 1880 when he was over with his first team. It was the return match with Yorkshire. I opened at the top end to Murdoch. George Freeman missed him off the first ball at short slip; Lockwood missed him off the second ball at point; off the third ball he was missed at the wicket by Pinder; off the fourth Lockwood caught him at point. He was thus missed three times in four balls and caught off the fourth. Rather a glorious innings!'

Charlie Turner's career started when Peate's ended and they never faced each other though it is of course feasible that they met on the circuit, particularly as in 1888 Turner took 283 first-class wickets, breaking Peate's existing record of 214 in 1882.

If Peate felt any pressure from Peel who was judged, quite reasonably, a better batsman, he did his best to make his case with a career-best performance against Surrey at Dewsbury. Peate hit 95 in the Yorkshire second innings after following on, which enabled them to hold out for a draw. It was evidently a lucky innings. Peate himself said: 'Walter Read was kind enough to carefully miss me before I had broken my duck. During the innings I hit a ball so high that the Surrey team were able to hold a committee meeting to decide who should attempt the catch. They called Diver from mid-off to mid-on to make it as he was supposed to be the safest catcher on the side. Then when he had carefully judged it, the ball fell three yards behind him.'

Despite high hopes, Yorkshire failed yet again to win the accolade of champions. They were disadvantaged by having a busy fixture list and though they won eight and drew four of their 16 games, it was their four lost games which counted against them in the days when the title was 'decided' upon fewest games lost. Nottinghamshire were deemed to be the champions, fair enough given their nine wins, one draw and no losses, but Middlesex's claim to second spot with four wins, three draws and three losses was hard to take. For Yorkshire it was the two players who had reputedly started the season under threat who performed best for them. Peate and Emmett were joint-leading wicket-takers, both with 61, with Emmett having the better average, 11.20 to Peate's 12.38. Peate was also in the top half of the batting stats with an average of 16.11. Significantly, the man earmarked to replace him, Bobby Peel, was only slightly ahead of him in the batting averages (16.6) and less effective with the ball (33 wickets at 14.6). The captain, Lord Hawke, had only played eight innings for a rather insipid average of 5.3. The *Yorkshire Post* summed it up as a disappointing season, citing the injury of Harrison and the decline of Ephraim Lockwood's batting as the reason though it noted that 'Hon. M.B. Hawke and several colts that were tried in different matches did not come up to expectation'.

A curious match was arranged after the county fixtures were over. Held at Lord's it pitted a Smokers XI against a Non-Smokers XI with proceeds going to the Cricketers Fund charity and this match has been granted first-class status. The Non-Smokers were led by W.G. Grace and Australian captain Billy Murdoch, the Smokers by Lord Harris and included Peate, Emmett and the best Australian bowler, Fred Spofforth. More than 11,000 spectators turned up over two days paying one shilling entrance fee thus boosting the charity by almost £600. Peate stole the show, despite the Smokers losing their wicketkeeper just before the match started. In his second spell he bowled 13 overs for ten runs and took six wickets. But the damage had already been done and the Non-Smokers won the match by nine wickets.

* * *

As 1885 dawned, Peate found himself elected to the committee of Guiseley Conservative Club, a position he was to maintain until his death. It is doubtful that he held any strong political views, the position being seen more as an honour (for both club and individual) and a mark of his status within his local community. He had also agreed to play another season for the ambitious local club based at Thornes, Hodgson and Simpson's. During April in four matches for this club he took 32 wickets at a cost of just 53 runs. He also turned out for Leeds Clarendon, who were captained by a local businessman who owned a number of hat shops in and around Leeds. This was S.R. Jackson, who was to become a friend and play a significant role in his later life.

Once again, Peate proved with his early-season exploits that he was far too good for even the top-ranked club cricketers. Despite opponents Armley including the Yorkshire opener Louis Hall as their professional, they were skittled out for just 27 with Peate taking 7-4 (though Hall was not among the victims and made 13).

The appearances piled up. He turned out for a side put together by Lancashire and England batsman Dick Barlow which also included Louis Hall, Ephraim Lockwood and Lancashire wicketkeeper Dick Pilling against an 18 of Ramsbottom District and for the Yorkshire team in the regular match against a team of hopeful triallists. Then it was down to Sussex for an appearance in Lord Sheffield's XI alongside W.G. Grace and Emmett playing against Shaw's XI (essentially the England side which had just returned from a tour of Australia including Ulyett, Bates and Peel). Alas for Lord Sheffield, this prestigious match on his country estate near Haywards Heath – for which he presumably paid the professionals handsomely for their services – was ruined by rain with only one innings per side. It is worth noting however that, for the only time, Peate and Grace bowled in tandem for a long spell and with remarkably similar figures, Peate with 2-58 in 55 overs and Grace 2-52 in 56 overs.

The *Nottingham Guardian* at this time printed a rather curious piece by an actor called J.S. Haydon who was then appearing at the city's Theatre Royal. It took the form of an acrostic poem (in which the first letter of each line spells out a word, in this case Edmund Peate):

Endowed with wondrous skill; known far and wide
Devoted to thy art; old Yorkshire's pride
Match after match, thy sterling worth hath shown
Unique thy style, a pitch and break thine own
No doubtful throw, but bowling fair and true

Destructive, scientific, graceful too
Prince thou of English bowlers say we all
Endowed by Spofforth, demon of the ball
Among our Yorkshire cracks long may we greet
Thy face, my friend, and see success complete
Enrolled on England's scroll with Edmund Peate

In May the real business of the county matches started and
Cricket magazine noted in its preview of the Yorkshire squad
that the 'genial' and 'cunning' Peate had started 1885 in his
usual deadly form. Peate's reputation was at its height. A
London photography studio called Wright and Co extensively
advertised a series of prints of famous photographs for the
not inconsiderable sum of £5 each. While most of the 23
featured were southern-based, Peate was included alongside
Tom Emmett, Bobby Peel and Billy Bates.

1885 was the season Yorkshire's captain, Lord Hawke,
made only one appearance for his county team, preferring
to concentrate on his captaincy of Cambridge University.
However, he had a ringside seat as the Louis Hall-led
Yorkshire coasted to victory over the students. Peate must
have loved taking Hawke's wicket in both Cambridge
innings against Yorkshire for 3 and 0. Lord Hawke must
have been impressed as he watched Peate take 5-12 in the
second innings.

However, despite the wealth of talent and predictions
that Yorkshire finally would be hailed as county champions,
they made a slow start. Peate scored 31 in the first innings
of Yorkshire's match against Sussex but rain ensured the
match ended in a draw. They then went down to an eight-
wicket defeat against Kent. Yorkshire's next match, against
MCC at Lord's, was to show the failings which dogged
Yorkshire and so frustrated Hawke. In their first innings
Yorkshire were skittled out for 69 in reply to MCC's 148.

However, in the second innings MCC were 72/3 before Nottinghamshire's Billy Gunn and Billy Barnes put on a stand of 330 for MCC. The reports mention some dismal fielding from Yorkshire but Peate was singled out for being the best bowler. Mercifully, the game was only scheduled for two days as the Derby took place the following day. Presumably Yorkshire's players (with the exception of the Methodist preacher Hall) made their way to Epsom to watch the race and the following day they were back at Lord's for the county fixture against Middlesex.

This was to spark a run of good form from Yorkshire which must have raised hopes that, at last, their promise would be realised. Middlesex were despatched by four wickets before Derbyshire were beaten by an innings at Huddersfield. In this match Peate somewhat rescued Yorkshire as he came in at number ten with Yorkshire 122/9 and scored 29 not out as his side amassed a winning total and took five wickets in each innings. Two draws against fiercest rivals Lancashire and Nottinghamshire were followed by four crushing wins – by an innings in the return against Nottinghamshire at Trent Bridge, by an innings over Gloucestershire, by 188 runs over Surrey and by eight wickets over Lancashire.

As well as his county matches, Peate was considered an essential element of any first-class match and thus he also turned out for the traditional Gentlemen v Players game, for the North v South and for the Yorkshire Gentlemen v Yorkshire Players matches. However, on the county scene, Yorkshire were unable to keep up their fine form. At Bradford, Gloucestershire were set a challenging target in a competitive match but when Peate bowled W.G. Grace for 1, the visitors abandoned all hope of victory and dropped the anchor to secure a draw. Two more draws, against Kent at Canterbury and Derbyshire at Derby followed, before Yorkshire lost at home to Middlesex at Bramall Lane and then drew with Sussex at Hove. At least they ended on a high with a victory over Surrey at The Oval.

The season was again a bit of an anti-climax for Yorkshire. Their 16 county fixtures included seven wins, seven draws and two losses. Nottinghamshire were again deemed champions, having played 12 matches, won six, drawn five and, crucially, having only lost one (albeit that innings defeat at home to Yorkshire). For Yorkshire, no-one had bowled more overs than Peate, no-one had taken more wickets. He had 61 victims at an average of 16.9. The averages were again topped by Emmett, with 58 wickets at 15.46. Both Peel and Bates were yet again behind Peate in both wickets and averages. The verdict of the *Yorkshire Post* upon the season was: 'The bowling has scarcely been so deadly as of yore, Ulyett's accident in June necessitating his giving up trundling till the last match – a very severe loss – while Peel and Peate have not approached their 1884 form. Bates has been expensive and Harrison and Preston uncertain and it is certainly a feather in the cap of the popular veteran Tom Emmett to find him top of the poll with an average of 15.46 per wicket.'

The season concluded with Lord Harris, the Kent and England captain (who would go on to become a notable administrator of cricket and president of MCC) writing an article in the magazine *Contemporary Review* in which he lauded the game of cricket. The article recommended young players to follow the example of three men: W.G. Grace for keeping his bat straight, Lancashire's Albert Hornby for his sheer determination and Peate, who 'goes on pitching the ball so near the same spot that at last it begins to look quite bare'.

He was at the pinnacle of his career. It was to come crashing down in little more than a year.

Chapter 7

Nemesis

LORD MARTIN Bladen Hawke of Towton dominates the early history of Yorkshire County Cricket Club. Adjectives frequently used to describe him include tyrannical, ruthless, dictatorial, stern and uncompromising. The commonly accepted view is that when he was appointed captain he described his team as 'ten drunks and a parson' and set about forcing a revolution, sweeping away the lax habits of his predecessors and imposing discipline and a ferocious will to win. The baronial seat of Towton, near Tadcaster, is the site of the bloodiest battle on British soil when 26,000 men, most of them Lancastrians, were routed by a Yorkist army led by the future King Edward IV in 1461. It is a thoroughly appropriate title for a man who reportedly gave no quarter. The 'ten drunks' story is a good one, but there is no record of him ever uttering the famous quote (sometimes given as a 'ten alecans'). It is more akin to the after-dinner anecdote of retired cricketers doing the annual club circuit. Yet it has the ring of truth about it. Louis Hall, a Methodist preacher and strict teetotaller, was presumably the parson in the team, leaving the rest as the drunks. As the first of the top players to be edged out of the team, Peate is suspect number one alecan.

Hawke's reputation has undergone something of a reappraisal in which the stern martinet character has been downplayed. A.A. Thompson, writing in the 1950s, 20 years after Hawke's death, may have been the first to concentrate on the achievements rather than the myth. He summarises him thus: 'The picture of him painted by some modern journalists as an arrogant peer, spurning with his cane a mob of ragged, trembling serfs labelled cricket professionals, is as false as it is ludicrous. When he took over the captaincy he found himself in charge of a body of talented, hearty and unruly buccaneers; when he retired he left as splendidly welded a county side as ever took the field and throughout that time he was more benevolent and less autocratic than Brian Sellers, Yorkshire's other great captain, could begin to be.'

Born at Gainsborough in Lincolnshire in 1860 – so five years younger than Peate – he thus became the 14th non-Yorkshireman to play for the county. He was the son of a parson himself, one who inherited the Hawke baronetcy when the main line ran out of male heirs and passed to the nearest cousin. The future seventh baron Hawke was educated at Newark, where he had the silly notion of being left-handed knocked out of him and learnt to bat the normal way – right-handed. Hawke was always a devout Christian and encouraged his players to go with him to church or join him in prayer. Not many did. At Eton he was a good cricketer – but not quite as good as Charles Studd, who would go on to play a fateful role with Peate in the 1882 Oval Test.

By the time Hawke went up to Cambridge in 1881 he was already well known in Yorkshire cricket circles turning out for the Yorkshire Gentlemen, which he slotted in between his hunting, shooting and church-going. For a while the Yorkshire Gentlemen deemed themselves the true representatives of cricket in Yorkshire and attempted to challenge the Sheffield stranglehold on the county game.

Hawke was too young to hold much sway in this power struggle, but it was to influence him later on as he sought to move power northwards.

It was the same Rev. Edmund Carter that discovered Peate who handed Hawke what is considered his Yorkshire debut, playing for the Yorkshire XI against MCC at the Scarborough Festival concluding the 1881 season. Hawke would have got his first glimpse of the Ulyett-Emmett-Lockwood-Peate quartet that pulled the strings of the professional Yorkshire side. Hawke scored 4 and 0 in his two innings. However, while Peate relied on his skill to force his way into the side, Hawke was earmarked for the future on account of his noble birth. The powerhouses on the Sheffield committee recognised this 21-year-old who was about to go to university as a man who might rein in the professional stranglehold.

Hawke made his debut for Yorkshire against county opposition in July 1882. Surrey were the opponents and Sheffield the venue. Hawke in his autobiography said that on arriving at the ground Emmett immediately submitted and offered him the captaincy, to which Hawke replied 'No, no, I prefer to play under you for the season and to pick up a few wrinkles.' It seems astonishing that a player of such prowess and experience as Emmett would have simply offered the captaincy to a 22-year-old making his county debut. However, it shows the elevated status of the amateur player who turned out for fun rather than be tainted by making money from his skills. At least the two classes existed side by side, which was more than can be said for the powers heading rugby football, who carried out a vicious persecution of working-class lads who asked simply for their wages to be met if they turned out for their local team. Hawke, despite his patrician background, was never to hold a grudge against professionals. He showed them respect and later on, when he had assumed control, he brought in a series of reforms which made their lot easier. In return they were to conform to his standards and expectations.

In April 1883 the Yorkshire committee meeting passed a resolution 'that T. Emmett be re-appointed captain until the Hon. M.B. Hawke plays'. Hawke was at Cambridge playing for the university side (and one assumes doing the odd bit of studying) for the early part of the season but the resolution was recognition that the county committee wanted a captain who was of the right breeding but could also hold down a place in the side. There had been a significant power swing in the committee rooms in 1883. Previously the club had been run by its president M.J. Ellison, agent to the Duke of Norfolk, who had put plenty of his own money into the Yorkshire team in its early years. The 14 members of the committee were all from Sheffield districts and were approved by Ellison, who also appointed the club secretary J.B. Wostinholm. However, in 1883 seven new members were added to the county committee representing Bradford, Leeds, York, Huddersfield, Dewsbury, Hull and Halifax. Sheffield still had its 14 members, but a split had been avoided.

Hawke admits to having a close relationship with Ellison, who he describes with Wostinholm as 'a jolly old pair of autocrats'. In his autobiography he states that whenever Yorkshire were playing in Sheffield he stayed with Ellison: 'He invariably entertained the visiting amateurs, giving them the best of everything, especially port.' Note, of course, that it was the amateurs who were entertained as Ellison's home; Peate and his fellow professionals would have to pay for their stay in a hotel. Hawke in the same passage says he never smoked until stumps were drawn and only drank water for lunch when playing. The inference is, of course, that others behaved differently.

Hawke's first appearance as captain was at Trent Bridge against Nottinghamshire on 2 July 1883. It was not an auspicious start. The captain scored 2 in the first innings and 3 in the second. He wasn't the only one to fail though as Yorkshire were all out for 61 in their first innings and only 61 from Ulyett in the second prevented an innings defeat, Notts winning by nine wickets. Hawke's biographer James Coldham wrote: 'The day when Hawke could snap his fingers and make Yorkshire dance to his tune lay far ahead ... while Emmett was in the team Yorkshire could never truly be Hawke's to command.' There was no animosity between the two – according to Coldham, 'The son of a peer of the realm and the incorrigible, lovable sporting brigand against all the odds formed an enduring affection and respect for each other, a friendship of a kind.'

In his autobiography Hawke speaks of Emmett's charm, his innate good nature and humour. By now he was past his 40th birthday but remained a key figure in the side for another five seasons. However, Hawke was no fan of professionals in charge, believing they could not have the same authority as an amateur. He cites one example – talent money. The committee would pay its professionals a sovereign (a gold coin worth, in theory, £1) for a score of 50 or six wickets but this meant 'sides suffered badly from a captain or a captain's chum being kept on to bowl too long in order to get his talent money'. Hawke will have noted this in action and the man who usually bowled most overs was Ted Peate.

Once Hawke had tightened his grip on Yorkshire, he began some of the reforms he deemed necessary to topple Nottinghamshire as the top county side. He abolished talent money. Instead he introduced a system of merit marks which were awarded dependent on factors such as the condition of the wicket, the weather, the state of the match, the quality of the opposition, in fact anything that Lord Hawke decided was worthy of 'merit'. He was the sole arbiter of merit marks and all were jotted down in his notebook. Peate taking six wickets on a wet pitch against a minor side like Derbyshire would be considered as just doing what was expected rather than worth a gold coin. Extra marks could be offered for other intangibles such as good fielding, enthusiasm and courage. Needless to say, these qualities were usually areas in which Peate was always requiring improvement. At the end of the season the team were invited to their captain's home, Wighill Park near Tadcaster, where the merit money was handed out in packets. For Hawke this distribution of brown envelopes was a 'red letter day' of his year and he thought it was for the players too. 'I often smiled at the various ways in which the lads opened [the envelopes] to see what they had earned, some surreptitiously as though fearing the others might see. During all the seasons I allocated marks I never had one grumble or remonstrance as to how I had doled out the rewards.'

Maybe not to his face, but one wonders what hard-bitten professionals who had come from working-class backgrounds thought in reality. They were summoned to the grand country house of a player who passed judgement on their efforts and doled out five shillings (25p) for each 'merit' mark the lord had deemed them worthy of. While the example of Peate's six wickets on a wet pitch against a minor team might now earn him nothing as opposed to a sovereign in the previous regime, a colleague might earn five shillings for what the captain considered a good catch among those six valueless wickets. Despite Hawke's confidence that his new system was welcome, it is hard to believe that behind the scenes there was no discontent.

Despite the poor start to his Yorkshire captaincy, Hawke guided the county to six wins and two draws in the latter part of the season, earning him a verdict of 'highly commended' by the county committee. However, it was not the springboard to better success. Indeed, Hawke only turned out for Yorkshire four times in 1884 as the captaincy devolved to the newly appointed vice-captain, Louis Hall. Part of the reason was his military involvement as he had been commissioned in the West Yorkshire militia, an early version of the Territorial Army. The following season saw even less of him as he completed his studies at Cambridge and concentrated on the captaincy of the university team. He failed to appear in any county match but a sample of his determination to win rather than play the part of a gentleman can be gleaned from his autobiography when he discusses his ending of the practice of picking some players to award them their representative blue as an honour rather than on merit: 'I have no patience with the sentimentality of giving a blue to a man because he is in his last year. To my mind it is absolutely childish unless he has made a remarkable advance in the current season. Places in the University Eleven should not go by favouritism but absolutely to the best.'

After graduating, Hawke was to return to his captaincy role in 1886 with Yorkshire. It soon became obvious that Hawke was not joking about having 'no patience with sentimentality'. The merit system was introduced and higher standards both on and off the field were demanded. Even so, Hawke retained his semi-adulatory relationship with Emmett, telling numerous tales of the way he amused colleagues. Emmett was notorious for bowling wides, much frowned upon in the Victorian era, and Hawke wrote in his autobiography: 'One year I thought it was getting too much so I said rather severely, "Tom, do you know how many wides you have bowled this season?" "Not the ghost of an idea, my Lord, how many?" "Forty-five," was my answer in reproving accents. "Then give me the ball my Lord and I'll soon earn talent money" was his unforgettable answer' – an echo of the talent system for 50 runs which Hawke scrapped.

Hawke even seems to have been mildly amused by Emmett's drinking – a latitude he did not share with other players. Hawke pokes fun at Emmett's large nose which developed the bluey-red hue of the seasoned drinker. On one occasion a supporter berated him for drinking too much beer. Emmett demanded to know who told him that and the spectator said Emmett's nose told him, to which Emmett replied: 'Then my nose is a blooming liar.' Another story related by Hawke is that during one Yorkshire game against Cambridge University, Emmett over-indulged at the dinner held at one of the colleges. 'Tom had dined so well as to induce him to say that he had drunk so much champagne that when he put his nose in the basin the next morning "it made the water fair phizz",' wrote Hawke. The enjoyment he recounts in telling his tales of Emmett suggests not just a sort of hero worship but also another side to him, a bit removed from the severe, autocratic, unbending image which has survived the decades.

Yet, as related in the previous chapter, there were murmurings as early as 1884 that Peate and Emmett were on their way out. The pair proved they were indispensable but by 1887, Hawke had moved from newcomer to leader, he had established his grip on the Yorkshire hierarchy and his authority was undisputed on and off the pitch. Then he shocked the cricketing world when he sacked Peate. The question was: Did Hawke target Peate as the chief instigator of all that was bad about Yorkshire or was there another reason?

Chapter 8

Sacked

TED PEATE'S first-class career slithered away remarkably quickly. Effectively it was killed in 1886 after he went from England's undisputed leading spin bowler to an uncertain future in a season and a bit. For many, such as James Coldham, Lord Hawke's biographer, he was the first to feel the force of the new captain's determination to whip his team into shape. Coldham writes: 'Peate's life was chaotic and if drink was partly to blame, his notoriety and the hero worship that attended it was his undoing … As long as he remained the premier bowler of his kind in the land Hawke tolerated his disruptiveness – and his "friends" – but when he slipped from his pedestal Bobby Peel was ready and waiting and Hawke dismissed Peate from Yorkshire cricket … His bowling powers were little diminished but he was a disruptive influence, a troublemaker and Hawke made an example of him.'

This follows the orthodox view on Peate. But was his behaviour 'disruptive'? Was he a 'troublemaker' surrounded by friends whose behaviour left much to be desired? Was drink to blame? Or was the truth that Peate's talent was draining fast and Hawke recognised a busted flush when he saw one?

At the start of the season few, if any, thought Peate was anything other than at the peak of his powers. *Cricket* magazine, in its preview of the 1886 season, called him 'Peate the Irresistible' and predicted that Yorkshire were as strong, if not stronger, than ever. On the home front, things seemed to be going well. He was now the father of two children under the age of five. His shop in Leeds seemed to be going well, the advertisements appearing regularly in the *Yorkshire Post* as his range expanded to include cigars and tobacco (alongside other sporting essentials). He was a personality, showing his rise in society by being elected to the committee of the Guiseley Conservative Club.

He warmed up for the new season by turning out for his hometown Yeadon but Yorkshire lost their first match of the county campaign at Surrey. From there Peate was to face the Australians yet again, this time representing the North at Old Trafford. As *Cricket* magazine pointed out, he always seemed to reserve his best for the Aussies. He followed up eight wickets in their first innings with four more in the second for match figures of 12-50. However, the wicket was wet and Peate was widely considered to be a specialist in such conditions. The final day was washed out, the match ending in a draw. This Australian tour of 1886 was, from an English point of view, a triumph with three Test victories, two of them by an innings. *Wisden*, however, described the tour as a 'feeble and spiritless thing'. The Australians were not a patch on their predecessors and *Wisden* damned them as having limited high-class batting, uncertain fielding, poor leadership and a lack of cohesion and enthusiasm in the team.

In the first Test (also at Old Trafford) on 7 July England won by four wickets. However, Peate's figures were unconvincing. Wicketless in the Australian first innings, he took just 1-45 in the second. Few realised it was to be his farewell appearance in the Test arena. His reputation as the best left-arm spin bowler in England was under attack from across the Pennines in the diminutive form of Johnny Briggs. Ironically Briggs was in the team at Old Trafford but did not bowl a single ball even though six bowlers were used. And while Peate was sending down 46 overs in the second innings at Old Trafford for his one success, at the other end Dick Barlow was wheeling away for 52 overs, to finish with 7-45. For the second Test at Lord's the selectors decided that Briggs could handle the left-arm spin and would contribute more runs. The *Yorkshire Post* was suitably unimpressed. 'For some reason neither Pilling nor Peate was included in the English eleven – the one the best wicketkeeper and the other the best and most scientific bowler in England. Murdoch [the Australian captain] said that Peate was immeasurably our best bowler and yet, because he has been unlucky for two or three weeks, he is not included in the eleven. Spofforth has of late enjoyed bad luck but the Australians have the brains not to exclude him.' However, the selectors' decision was justified as Briggs took 5-29 then 6-45 as England romped to an innings and-106-run victory. It was the end of Test cricket for Peate.

As June started the county season, Peate took 9-21 in another rain-affected draw against Sussex at Huddersfield. Unfortunately, the new captain Hawke was still not in the side, making his first appearance in the next match against Middlesex when Peate took a solid 5-110 across both innings. A pattern had been set as Peate was acceptable but not spectacular in matches against Kent, Cambridge University, Derbyshire and Nottinghamshire, all of them now under the noble lord's gimlet eye. He took five wickets in the Nottinghamshire first innings but none in the second. What must Lord Hawke have thought when Peate went in to bat at his customary number ten with Yorkshire still requiring 36 to win at Nottingham? He moved rapidly to 22 and there was a chance of a thrilling win – but Peate ran himself out and the game was lost. Caught or bowled while going for the runs would have been more acceptable than to run himself out!

After Peate's final Test appearance, there was a chance to impress against his favourite opponents Australia but this time both he and his county were unimpressive as the tourists chalked up a comfortable win at Sheffield. Yorkshire were finding wins hard to come by despite the pre-season predictions and in a narrow loss at Old Trafford Peate only managed one wicket in the game. Still, no-one else did any better other than Emmett, who took nine of the 16 Lancastrian wickets to fall. The Australians were again lined up to play a second game against Yorkshire at Huddersfield in late July but rain meant very little play on the first two days.

By now Yorkshire were in a rut and *Cricket* magazine printed a poem bemoaning their failure to sparkle. Matches against Gloucestershire and Lancashire were ruined by rain but surely wet wickets were Peate's forte. However, against Lancashire, at Dewsbury, the visitors only faced one innings due to a washout for the best part of the first two days and Peate was wicketless. At the other end Billy Bates took 6-19 and Hawke brought Peate out of the attack and tried Emmett. He was rewarded with four quick wickets as Lancashire were all out for 53. It was another demerit mark for Peate as far as Hawke was concerned.

At Canterbury, Yorkshire lost again and Peate failed to take a wicket but at Sheffield there was a hope of a revival when the mighty Nottinghamshire were the visitors. Again rain-affected, Notts only batted the once, Peate taking 4-29 and Emmett 5-49. However, Hawke made his move. It was halfway through August and Yorkshire had only won one match, against the minnows of Derbyshire. The axe fell on Ted Peate and batsman Fred Lee, another with a reputation for enjoying his beer. Hawke was looking to shore up the batting and Albert Ward replaced Lee while all-rounder Saul Wade, who was in his first season, was handed the baton for Peate's bowling duties. *Cricket* magazine was surprised, commenting: 'Peate's absence is particularly noteworthy as the first occasion he has been omitted from the county side for some years.'

In his autobiography, Hawke takes full responsibility for sacking Peate, although he makes it clear that he had the wholehearted backing of the 'two jolly old autocrats' Michael Ellison, the president, and Joseph Wostinholm, the secretary. 'He [Ellison] had a dry way of encouraging Wostinholm, who was a perfect Tartar ... They were both invariably goodness itself to me and as loyal as could be. Neither could do enough for me and when I dismissed Peate, and years after Peel, they stood by me and supported decisions which I have never regretted, however reluctant I was to take steps so drastic but absolutely necessary for the morale of my team and the good of the game.'

A measure of the shock back in Yorkshire caused by Peate's dropping from the team to play Middlesex can be gleaned from the following letter published by the *Yorkshire Post*: 'I was very much surprised to see that Peate, who is undoubtedly the first slow bowler in the world, has been left out of the match against Middlesex on Monday next .... Why he should be put on one side I cannot imagine. Even with all his bad fortune this year in the matter of bowling, I believe that all who have been present at the Yorkshire matches will agree with me that Peate's bowling has been treated with more marked respect than any other trundler from the county and I think the committee have made a grave mistake. Any county in England, bar Notts, will be glad to get him and they will pay him even more than he gets from the county of his birth.'

Albert Ward was not a great success (although he did far better subsequently when he moved to Lancashire) and the man he replaced, Lee, was to last on Yorkshire's books for another four seasons. However, Peate's cause was not helped when his replacement Wade took 6-26 in the Middlesex first innings plus two more in the second as Yorkshire won by an innings and 196 runs. Emmett, now 45 years old, took ten wickets in the match.

It wasn't the end, but it was the beginning of the end for Peate. Yorkshire finished the season well, with wins over Gloucester and Derbyshire and much the better of a draw with Sussex at Hove. Peate was brought back in September for the final match of the Scarborough Festival but took only two wickets in an easy win for MCC. He had slipped to third in the averages and wicket-taking – ill luck according to the newspapers. For the record, Wade's 32 wickets for 299 at an average of 9.34 put him top, Emmett had 96 wickets at 11.1 and Peate 39 wickets at 14.2.

Cricket magazine on 23 September 1886 published an interview with Fred Spofforth, nicknamed The Demon Bowler, who was one of the first ten Australian cricketers to be inducted into the Australian Cricket Board's 'Hall of Fame' along with the likes of Don Bradman, Keith Miller, Dennis Lillee and Ray Lindwall. The interview was about the art of bowling and here is what one of the finest ever Australian bowlers had to say after declining to give an opinion on the best English batsman in the game: 'As a bowler, and judging with a critical eye, in my own opinion Peate is far the best and most dangerous English bowler. As I have said about myself, some find they can play Peate better than a much less formidable bowler. But him I place first, though I must ask you to say that I only give this as my own individual opinion, though I express it very strongly. He constitutes the first class in the lists; there are many competitors for the second, whom I need not enumerate.' This glowing summary from an Australian great was published just as Yorkshire were turning their back on Peate.

The 1887 season, Peate's last with Yorkshire, dawned with big questions over his place in the team. Most fans and the press put his indifferent 1886 down to bad luck and viewed his dropping from the team as more than harsh. Peate was named in the team to play the colts, the pre-season trial. He was also playing for Yeadon and Hawke selected Peate to play for Yorkshire in the traditional match against MCC at Lord's. Yorkshire were well beaten and lost by nine wickets with no bowler having any great success.

From there it was on to the first county match at Huddersfield against Warwickshire (not then considered first-class opposition). Yet again much play was lost due to rain and Warwickshire held on for a draw. They were 35/7 in their second innings and only just avoided an innings defeat. Lord Hawke absented himself from the match but he would have studied the card and noted that Emmett had taken 7-30 in the first innings and Joseph Preston (ironically another Yeadon man) 3-15. Peate, the wet wicket specialist, failed to take a scalp despite bowling 15 overs. The second innings was more telling. With three of England's finest spinners in the team in Peel, Bates and Peate, only the first two were used. Peate stood on the sidelines watching as his great rivals took all seven wickets to fall for 35 runs.

At some point after this, Hawke must have told Peate that he was finished. There is no 'smoking gun', no letter, no diary entry, no committee minute. All we are left with are Hawke's personal recollections, written down almost a quarter of a century after Peate's death. His autobiography first pays tribute to Peate, describing his eight Surrey wickets for just five runs as 'the very best bowling feat to which I ever fielded'. He continues: 'Peate was blessed with the most perfect action of any man I have seen deliver the ball and, to look at him, you would have thought he was the very last man ever to have deputised in a troop of Clown Cricketers. Another curious feature was that he began as a very fast bowler, though throughout his career in big cricket his pace was slow ... Nobody ever bowled more with his head but his only principle, with all his variations, was always to bowl with a length – a golden rule he acquired from watching Alfred Shaw. One of my saddest tasks was to dismiss him from the Yorkshire eleven. But he bore me no grudge and whenever I subsequently ran across him invariably he greeted me with the old familiar smile and same slow, spontaneous "Good morning, my Lord. I hope you are as well as I am."'

And that is it. No explanation, no justification. We are left to read between the lines. For example, what is the significance of the word 'dismiss'? Does Hawke use it in the exclusively modern sense of 'sack', with some sense of shame, or does he mean it in the less pejorative sense of cast aside, choose an alternative?

The commonly accepted view is that Peate was a bad influence who was prone to drink. There were hints at the time – the verdict in *Wisden*'s obituary is commonly cited as evidence of his dissolute behaviour: 'Without using a harsh word, it may fairly be said that he would have lasted longer if he had ordered his life more carefully.' As we have already seen, Coldham's autobiography of Lord Hawke is harsh on Peate. Derek Hodgson, in his *Official History of Yorkshire County Cricket Club*, talks of his 'disorderly conduct' while Anthony Woodhouse in his exhaustive *History of Yorkshire CCC* also refers to Peate's drinking: 'His dropping may have been because the discipline in the side was lax and he had put on weight ... Not much good as a batsman and unreliable in the field, he was known to drink a little too but the fact that Peel was able to take his position may have been the real reason.' It all plays into the 'ten drunks and a parson' quip supposedly made by Lord Hawke.

A flavour of the changing attitude from the top can be gleaned from the speech given by county president Michael Ellison at the 1889 annual meeting, two years after Peate had been disposed of. Yorkshire had started the season with high expectations but had a dismal season; it was a 'lamentable failure' said Ellison and there were loud grumbles from many supporters about why Peate was not in the team. Ellison, in analysing the poor results, did not refer directly to Peate, but it shows the sort of thinking in the Yorkshire hierarchy. The report of his speech given in *Cricket* magazine is worth quoting at length:

'For this result [i.e. the 'lamentable season'] a large number of people who call themselves supporters of cricket were responsible. The great difficulty with which they had had to contend arose from what he might call "the demon drink". They had had to put out of the team one upon whom they had relied as a tower of strength for a great many years and at a critical time they had to suspend another. In a great measure these occurrences were caused by those who called themselves supporters of cricket who came to the ground and who could not see a professional cricketer without wanting to give him a glass of drink. They never thought that if they gave him a glass a thousand others would want to do the same. If the grateful professional accepted the offer of one man and refused that of another he made himself enemies. People who have done this have been remonstrated with.'

This was one of the greatest difficulties with which they had to contend and he wished its serious nature would be borne home to everyone who frequented the ground. The most serious thing they could do to a professional cricketer was to offer him a drink. It not only imperilled his immediate advantage in destroying his chance of being a member of the county team but it endangered his future interests when he came to apply for a benefit.

This is the clearest explanation yet for Peate's dismissal. He was the biggest name to be axed and is most likely the player referred to who was a tower of strength and had to be put out of the team because of the demon drink. It is interesting too that Ellison blames the spectators for the problem – they were too keen to buy their hero a beer and he was too weak to refuse.

The failure of the Yorkshire team in 1889, when they lost 12 matches was pivotal for Hawke's captaincy and resulted in a spate of sackings. As Rev. R.S. Holmes put it: 'At the close of this season the curtain fell on the cricketing of four men who seemed at one time certain to take a foremost place: I refer to Fred Lee, Saul Wade, Irwin Grimshaw and Joe Preston – cricketers of whom it may be said in all charity that they had only themselves to blame for the disappointment they proved to all followers of county cricket.' This is far more condemnatory of their behaviour than Holmes, a guru of Yorkshire cricket writing, had delivered on Peate. Indeed Holmes was to remain a supporter of Peate into the next decade, writing articles querying his hasty dismissal from the Yorkshire team. Interestingly, Saul Wade was the man who had initially replaced Peate in the county team while Joe Preston was, ironically like Peate, from Yeadon. Lord Hawke in his autobiography throws off all restraint in his verdict of Preston: 'He was an irresponsible individual who, had he possessed the least self-restraint, might have become one of the finest cricketers Yorkshire ever produced … but he had too many friends.' Those friends again, forcing drink into the hands of naïve professionals. Joe Preston lasted only a year after being sacked by Yorkshire. In November 1890 he died from pneumonia.

If we see Peate as the first victim of Hawke clearing out the bad influences in 1887, a second wave was to follow in 1889. And yet, and yet ...

There is no recorded evidence of Peate being drunk. It is all hints, rumours and subtle digs. It is clear that Peate did like a beer but was he worse than any others in the team? There is at least equal evidence that Tom Emmett and George Ulyett were more likely to let their hair down than Peate. Emmett was to be forced out of the county game in 1888 at the age of 47; Ulyett was to carry on until 1893 until he too, at the age of 42, retired. Ulyett, of course, had survived that gambling controversy in Australia and has gone down in folklore as 'Happy Jack' for his sunny demeanour and happy-go-lucky attitude to life. Coldham quotes Ulyett as saying after a game at Cambridge against the university, 'That's the best spot of eddication [sic] as ever I sat eyes on, for them young fellers get taught to drink beer from morning to night with baccy thrown in.' He also describes Ulyett as 'breaking bowlers' hearts with the same abandon that he sank pints of beer'. Emmett also could take a less than serious attitude to life and was renowned for his joking. It was he who when caught in heavy seas in the Bay of Biscay en route to Australia quipped 'someone forgot to bring out the heavy roller'.

There is a photograph of Ephraim Lockwood, Ted Peate, George Ulyett and Tom Emmett taken at Cambridge in which they are dressed up as graduates, all wearing mortar boards and gowns. It is likely that the occasion was the Yorkshire match against Cambridge University which started on 24 May 1882 but was ended by rain on the final day. It is not inconceivable that the four Yorkshire stars from humble backgrounds would have thought it a splendid jape to dress themselves up as academics. They had the opportunity, as they waited in vain for the rain to stop and ground to clear, to have wandered into a photographer's studio in the town. The Victorians had a passion for having their photograph taken and almost always wore their very best suit or dressed up in fancy clothing. Photographers were only too keen to satisfy this booming demand and what could be more natural in the famous university town than to dress up as one of the elite academics? One thing for certain is that Lord Hawke, who was in the Cambridge University team facing the Yorkshire side, would have been highly unamused at the breach of protocol. For him, wearing academic gowns to which they were not entitled would have been a grave lack of form. It was another black mark against the professionals who made up the Yorkshire side but seemed to lack a respect for etiquette.

The photograph is in typical Victorian studio style. The four cricketers are not smiling (due to the length of exposure required it was hard to bear a smile for long enough so a serious pose was the normal style). On the left is Lockwood, wearing a white gown which makes him look more like a vicar than a don. He is not looking at the camera but leaning forward staring at an open book as if reading. Peate is next, staring intently at the camera with his fingers entwined across his lap maybe with a bat handle between. Ulyett is next, the only one standing, in a relaxed pose, while the captain Emmett is on the right, both hands resting on an open book. There is the hint of a smile on his face, as if he has great satisfaction in poking fun at the privileged background of his opponents who were back at the ground. This was an unusual match for Peate. *Cricket* magazine expressed its surprise that 'the singular feature [of the Yorkshire bowling] was the ill success of Peate who delivered 40 overs for no wicket'.

If Hawke did take exception to the picture, no action was taken, at least officially. He was to rely heavily on Ulyett and Emmett for many years. So Peate, Ulyett and Emmett appear to have been a triumvirate of senior players of extreme talent but inveterate drinkers who some blamed for taking a cavalier attitude to the game. The upshot of this approach was that Yorkshire lost games they should have won. However, why was Peate the only one who was cast aside while Ulyett and Emmett were allowed to linger on into their 40s? And the man who took over from Peate as the slow bowler, Bobby Peel, has a far worse disciplinary record.

Another accusation levelled at Peate is of being a disruptive influence but there is no real evidence of this. He may have over-estimated his value to the side when expressing his opinions but it is only hinted at in Lord Hawke's autobiography. The character of Ulyett and Emmett suggest that they were so laid back as to go with the flow. Peate, on the other hand, may have kicked back a little and resented the way a lax attitude which had been perfectly acceptable for six seasons at Yorkshire was suddenly being condemned. Another explanation is that Ulyett and Emmett, one already past 40, the other rapidly approaching it, were canny enough to realise that their careers were approaching the end and were only too happy to bend a little. Peate had only just turned 30 and was widely acclaimed as the finest slow bowler in the game. Who was this young upstart from a privileged background who had already taken action to cut Peate's income by introducing his own system of delivering so-called merit money? Peate's place in the team looked unshakeable; Hawke on the other hand was never quite in the first rank of batsmen, a sort of 19th-century equivalent of Mike Brearley, the England captain of the early 1980s – a great captain, an average player. Could Peate have paid the price for grumbling in the background?

So posterity has decreed that Peate was sacked for a combination of indiscipline and intoxication. However, I feel that this explanation plays too much to the caricature of Lord Hawke as a humourless martinet who looked down his nose at the working-class oiks who challenged his authority. Instead, is it not possible that Hawke was a great captain who was one of the very first to recognise that, at the top level, Peate was on the slide? And when he pondered the future, he saw that there was one, possibly two replacements who were as good and possibly better?

There are several newspaper references at this point to Peate's fitness. He had suffered a sprained ankle which had kept him out of the Yorkshire team and in his obituaries some newspapers referred to a blow on the inside of his knee which prevented his comeback. The best example was the *Wharfedale Observer* of 16 March 1900 which makes it clear that his Yorkshire days were far from considered to be over when he was dropped. It states, 'His career as a first-class cricketer was cut short while he was yet in his prime, a nasty blow on the inside of the knee joint having serious effects and preventing him standing the strain of three days' continuous hard cricket necessitated by county matches. An occasional reappearance in an important game proved that Peate, for years after his place in the county eleven had been filled by Peel in 1887, still possessed all his old skill and remarkable ability to weigh up the opposing batsman but always brought home to him the conviction that the damage to his knee had closed for him the portals of first-class cricket. A few seasons back he had an invitation from the Yorkshire County Committee to play in certain matches but after several days' practice in local cricket he broke down and had regretfully to decline the honour.'

Further evidence that Hawke did not sack Peate for misdemeanours can be found in a rather curious report in the *Yorkshire Post* of 6 June 1887. The article reviews the Yorkshire line-up which the author considered was in serious need of strengthening in the batting department – Peate of course was not renowned as a batsman despite the *Yorkshire Post*'s perennial optimism that deep down he was capable of batting higher up the order. The article welcomes the addition of some new blood and states 'Peate has himself asked to be left out'. There is no corroboration of this declaration but taken with the later comments about his knee injury and struggle to last three full days of the county game in which he was called on to bowl 40–50 overs in a day, it is evidence that Peate's exclusion from Yorkshire was down to physical decline rather than temperamental weakness.

One thing we do know is that by this point Peate's eyesight was fading. Soon after his return to club cricket he was wearing spectacles while playing and contemporary reports confirm that his vision was going. Rev. R.S. Holmes, who held a torch for Peate deep into the next decade, blamed his decline not on Hawke's search for discipline but on this failing eyesight. Certainly, Yorkshire seemed to take a cavalier approach to fielding which Hawke was keen to improve. Holmes wryly commented: 'The team was very slack in the field; indeed their weakness in this respect became so notorious that it was said that Yorkshiremen were far too polite to run a man out.' Peate was never a renowned fielder. He was a big, heavy man – though portly at this stage would be overstating it – who lacked the nimbleness and agility which is essential to the modern game. In fact, in July 1884 the *Yorkshire Post*, in response to a reader's query, gives Peate's weight as 11 stones 12 pounds. For a tall man this does not suggest being overweight. In contrast Ulyett weighed, according to the newspaper, 'about 13 stones'. True, Peate clearly had an issue with his weight in his last decade but he must have gone rapidly to seed in just a couple of years if Hawke considered weight a factor in his decision.

If Hawke really did 'sack' Peate, then he seems remarkably open to the notion of him making a comeback. On 23 May 1887 Peate was in the Yorkshire team at Lord's for the traditional match against MCC. Hawke captained the side and gave him every chance, keeping him on for 32.2 overs which was more than his rivals Bates, Peel and indeed Wade while only Emmett was given more. It was the same story in the second innings of this two-day drawn match when Yorkshire sent down only 20 overs but Peate was handed eight of them. MCC had much the better of the game and Peate only took one wicket, though no-one returned particularly effective figures. He was back in the side later in the week for a match against Warwickshire. At the time Warwickshire were not considered a first-class side (they achieved that status in 1894) but did have fixtures against the likes of Yorkshire and Surrey. Alas, against what Yorkshire would have looked upon as inferior opponents, Peate was wicketless. That was his swansong, his final Yorkshire match against another county though not quite his final appearance in a Yorkshire side. At the end of June he was in the Yorkshire team which took on – and lost to – a Liverpool and District XI. Hawke gave the game a miss and did not see Peate take his one wicket in the two innings. There was, however, an unsavoury incident which, if reported back to Hawke, would have lowered Peate's stock further. He claimed a catch off his own bowling and the batsman walked only to be called back by Louis Hall, the captain, because it was a 'bump' ball which had hit the ground immediately after contact with the bat. If Peate knew that, it can only be seen as a desperate attempt to try to inflate his figures from a man who sensed the end was nigh. Either way, it would not have gone down well.

Peate spent the rest of 1887 playing for Yeadon, turning out for Yorkshire in August against a Newcastle 18 at Gosforth (unlike the Liverpool fixture this is not considered to be a first-class match) and having one-off engagements for other club sides. He finished the season with 90 wickets for his home town club at an average of 4.72. One man convinced that Peate still had what it took at the top level was a young wicketkeeper called David Hunter. He was to go on to be Yorkshire's wicketkeeper for 20 years during the glory years of Hawke's County Championship-winning sides and although he was emerging at the very tail end of Peate's career, he still had no doubt about the veteran's skills. Hunter was another who rated him at the very top: 'Peate was the finest left-arm bowler I ever saw. He had a beautiful action and was extraordinarily accurate, seldom, if ever losing his length.'

There is evidence therefore that Hawke had growing doubts about Peate's ability to play at the lofty standards he had set over the previous seven seasons. If so, he would have weighed up his options and considered alternatives. He did not have to look far. Yorkshire were blessed with not just Peate but his rivals Billy Bates and Bobby Peel. They were already established members of the Yorkshire team; however, it was rare that all three played together and the accepted view was that Peate plus one would form the spin bowling attack. From 1885 onwards, Hawke, like his namesake bird of prey, would have been paying close attention to the trio before swooping down. Peate's relatively undistinguished season of 1886 was the signal to strike.

* * *

Billy Bates was a few months younger than Peate yet had burst on to the first-class scene two years before the Yeadon man. This possibly was due to the fact that he was a product of the famous Lascelles Hall production line. This club, founded in 1825 near Huddersfield, boasted that it produced more cricketers for the county than any other rival. Its fixture list was envied by other clubs as it contained matches against All England, Yorkshire, Surrey, Yorkshire Gentlemen and a number of public schools. At one time six Lascelles Hall old boys were in the Yorkshire team. Derek Hodgson, in his *Official History of Yorkshire County Cricket Club*, states that there were 21 Lascelles Hall cricketers who appeared for Yorkshire. Those mentioned in this book from the club were John Thewlis, Ephraim Lockwood, Allen Hill plus of course Bates. He was only 19 when his first recorded appearance for the club was made against the North of England but he had already featured in less prestigious games whose record is now lost. Hodgson states that he was considered a child cricketing prodigy and his peers were reluctant to let him bat as they knew they could not get him out so he concentrated on developing slow off breaks. Against the North he was not entrusted with the bowling and batted at number 11 in a two-day drawn match, so it was a Lascelles Hall fixture against Yorkshire in September 1876 which probably brought him more to the attention of the county club. This time he was opening the batting and scored 39 against a team including Yorkshire captain Emmett and stalwarts Ulyett, Lockwood, Pinder and Hall. Again he did not bowl. At the same time, Peate was a clown cricketer.

That led to a trial match against Nottinghamshire Colts in May 1877 in which he top scored with 22 in a Yorkshire Colts first-innings total of 56 and then took 7-15 as Notts were all out for 34. A week later he was heading down to Lord's with the Yorkshire first team. He acquitted himself well. From now on, Bates was a regular member of the Yorkshire team. He was with Peate on the tour to Australia in early 1882 and would go on to make 15 Test appearances against the Australians – though all of them came Down Under as he was never picked for a home Test. He does, however, have the distinction of being the first Englishman to achieve a hat-trick in Test cricket, achieved in January 1883 in Melbourne (the tour where, for whatever reason, Peate stayed at home).

Bates earned a reputation as a snappy dresser and was nicknamed 'The Duke'. Ephraim Lockwood referred to him as 'The Dashing One'. Cricket author Peter Thomas said of him, 'Everything that Billy Bates did was in grand and splendid style. He dressed superbly in days when cricket professionals were not renowned for their sartorial elegance. He bowled at times brilliant medium to slow off breaks.' While he was, compared to some in the side, not one of the main practical jokers in the squad, he did have his moments. Tom Emmett, in his interview with Pullin, tells the story of how Bates got the better of him in a bet he rashly struck playing against Gloucestershire in 1879. Gloucestershire needed just 27 runs to beat Yorkshire and had eight wickets, one of them W.G. Grace, in hand. After saying Yorkshire's chances were slim, Bates piped up to ask what odds he would give. When Emmett said 50 to one, Bates handed him a shilling. Peate and Bates got to work and quickly ran through the remaining batsmen to secure a seven-run victory for Yorkshire and Emmett handed over the 50 shillings (or at least he says he did – in Ulyett's interview with Pinder he tells the same story but adds 'the players had a little meeting among themselves after the game and told Bates that he ought to accept 30 shillings, which he did').

So what was Lord Hawke's view of Peate's great rival? He had a high opinion of his batting, writing in his autobiography, 'I do not think Yorkshire ever had a more attractive bat than Billy Bates. Indeed, until Hobbs came along, I think he was the most engaging of all professional run-getters. He never let a ball go by, he was always after it as he was in the field, where he covered a lot of ground. He could lay on, to be sure!' However, Hawke makes no comment about his bowling.

If Hawke was relying on statistics, we turn to R.S. Holmes' authoritative history of the club to compare the bowling records of the two playing for Yorkshire:

1879 – Peate 75 wickets at 12.44 average, Bates 65 at 11.06; 1880 – Peate 139 at 11.61, Bates 74 at 14.82; 1881 – Peate 139 at 12.73, Bates 81 at 16.93; 1882 – Peate 165 at 11.19, Bates 70 at 18.02; 1883 – Peate 70 at 12.65, Bates 51 at 16.05; 1884 – Peate 81 at 12.12, Bates 27 at 24.33; 1885 – Peate 80 at 15.96, Bates 66 at 20.03; 1886 – Peate 68 at 13.42, Bates 76 at 16.14. From these figures alone, the impartial viewer would deduce that bowling-wise Bates was not in Peate's class. In every year, except the critical one of 1886, Peate had taken more wickets. In every year except 1879, Peate's debut season when his supporters might reasonably argue he was just finding his feet, Bates had a far inferior average. There was no argument that Bates was the better batsman, though his average was not incredibly better than Peate's. In five of the eight seasons from 1879 to 1886, Peate's average was only seven below that of his rival's.

With Peate shown the exit door for the 1887 season, Bates played in 24 matches for Yorkshire, his highest ever tally, but Hawke's gamble did not really pay off. He took 48 wickets with a career-worst average of 26.89. And if Hawke had Bates in mind as a longer-term replacement for Peate, he was to be cruelly thwarted as Bates had an even sadder ending to his career than Peate. He was selected to tour Australia at the end of the 1887 season. Confusingly two touring teams were taken out, one organised by those masters of tour operations, Shaw and Shrewsbury, and the other by Middlesex professional George Vernon. The latter squad was captained by Hawke and included the man in whom he had placed his confidence, Bates. In Shaw's squad were two other Yorkshiremen – Ulyett and Preston. Shaw's team games against Australia are recognised as Test matches by Cricket Archive but *Wisden* lists only the match in Melbourne, when the two sides combined, as the sole Test of the tour. It was while preparing for this Melbourne fixture that Bates was struck in the eye from a straight drive while practising his bowling in the nets. It was a serious injury that ended his career.

Vernon's side was dogged with ill luck. The organiser, himself a leading batsman, fell down a gangplank coming off the boat and suffered severe injuries; Walter Read, another batsman, sprained his ankle, and then the captain Lord Hawke returned home after receiving news that his father had died. However, Bates' injury was the worst and it was feared he would lose his eye. It is said that, knowing his cricketing career was over, he tried to kill himself on the journey home. A little over a year later, Bates appeared before Huddersfield magistrates 'greatly altered and looking very pale and thin' charged with attempted suicide. The court was told by a doctor that Bates had attempted to cut his throat on 24 January 1889 and he had found him with a bad wound and severe loss of blood. However, he was now recovering his strength but was still very much depressed. The prosecution was brought by the West Riding Chief Constable, who told the court that Bates was suffering business difficulties and had been extremely depressed. He was still in a fragile state of mind and would need close attention from his friends if the court took the course of action he was to propose. The *Huddersfield Daily Examiner* reported the Chief Constable as saying: 'Under the circumstances seeing that Bates was in such a state of mind at the time as to be scarcely responsible for his acts and that no good could possibly accrue from continued persecution of him and with the hope that the result of his act would prevent Bates repeating the offence, he [the Chief Constable] had to ask that the bench would allow him to withdraw the charge and at the same time express a hope that Bates would recover his mind and physical strength and never again be found in a similar position.' After hearing that Bates' brother had undertaken to look after him, the bench agreed to dismiss the charge. Bates left the court with his wife and brother and was taken home in a cab.

The cricketing community rallied round. A benefit fund was set up to help Bates out of his financial difficulties and Louis Hall voluntarily gave up the benefit he had been awarded in return for the Yorkshire committee organising a subscription and setting it in motion with a £50 donation. The fund eventually raised more than £1,000 and Bates opened a sports shop in his home town which appears to have struggled. He did not disappear entirely from view and turned out for his home club Lascelles Hall. The *South Australian Register* newspaper in August 1892 reported that 'the once universally popular Billy Bates ... after beginning the season with some good scores for his native Lascelles Hall, went out with the Leek club and signalised his engagement there by scoring 88 runs against Bollington, afterwards capturing three wickets for 18 runs'. His time in Staffordshire lasted only one season.

Bates' career is remarkable because of the parallels with Peate's. They were born weeks apart in 1855, and often bowled in tandem as Yorkshire's spin attack. Their first-class career ended involuntarily one year apart and they died within weeks of each other in 1900. Both died in remarkably similar circumstances – both inadvisedly went out in bad weather and caught a cold which turned into pneumonia. In Bates' case it was while attending the funeral of fellow Yorkshire cricketer and Lascelles Hall man John Thewlis on a bitterly cold day. The two lie side by side in Kirkheaton cemetery, Huddersfield. Even their first-class career statistics are similar. According to Cricket Archive, Peate sent down 47,025 balls, Bates 42,852. Peate gave away 14,517 runs, Bates 14,979. Only on wickets and average does Peate pull away – 1,076 wickets to Bates' 874 giving Peate an average of 13.49 compared to Bates' 17.13. One other crucial difference is also worth pointing out – Bates was given a testimonial after his career ended which raised more than £1,000 – Peate got nothing.

If Lord Hawke's plan for Bates to be the long-term Peate replacement was thwarted, he would have had higher hopes for Bobby Peel. Two years younger than both of them, his first-class career had begun three years after Peate's. He got his call-up for Yorkshire when Peate's sprained ankle ruled him out of the match against Surrey in July 1882. The youngster took 4-46 and then 5-83 and was retained in the side for the next game, against Australia at Dewsbury. This was the first time the two played together for Yorkshire and Peate must have had any complacency about his place in the team knocked out of him. While he took 0-44, Peel took 6-41. Here was a real rival who, like Bates, also fancied himself with the bat. From this point Peel was a regular in the team.

Peel was another whose drinking feats are almost always mentioned in tandem with his cricketing exploits. David Frith, in his book about the 1894/95 tour *The First Great Test Series* states that, after following on in the first Test at Sydney, England set Australia 177 to win and they were 113/2 on the fifth day of a match which was played without a time limit, continuing until a result was achieved. Heavy rain fell overnight but several English players, believing the game lost, had been boozing far into the early hours. Peel was still drunk and was stuck under a cold shower before being sent out to do his magic on a wet wicket. Frith relates: 'Peel, as oblivious as any to the night's rainfall, at first thought someone had watered the wicket. As it gradually dawned on his befuddled brain that England were back in with a chance he is supposed to have said to his skipper, "Give me the ball Mr Stoddart and I'll get the boogers out before loonch."' He took six wickets in a celebrated England victory.

The most famous story of Peel's excessive drinking surrounded his sacking. In a notorious episode at Bradford in 1897, Peel was still drunk and unable to take the field for the start of play against Middlesex. He had also been 'indisposed' for the final day of the previous match against Lancashire. Whatever Peate's drinking habits, no-one ever accused him of being too drunk to play, yet Peel played from Yorkshire from 1883 to 1897 and received a benefit in 1893 from the Roses fixture. There is some dispute as to whether when he finally appeared at Bradford he actually urinated on the wicket, some cricket historians seeing this as a later embellishment. Hawke led Peel off the pitch and into retirement. Like Peate, the story has been polished down the years and many cricket historians believe the incident never happened, though they concede that he may well have swayed a bit and slurred his speech. The newspaper reports of the time do not note any untoward behaviour though they were more discreet in those days. It seems as though Peel was, in the words of some newspapers, 'unable to do himself justice' with the ball. Lord Hawke left the field and was spotted conferring with committeemen and after the game was finished it was announced that Peel was suspended for the rest of the season.

The *Leeds Daily News* interviewed Peel, who admitted to having a couple of gins before the game and agreed that he had slipped over a couple of times in the field but produced for the reporter a pair of boots showing three studs missing and said this was the cause of his unsteadiness. He was shocked by his suspension and said: 'I never heard a word of complaint, nor ever expected a whisper of that kind until, at the close of the match, when Mr Wostinholm [Yorkshire's secretary] paid me my money, he said, "Peel, I am sorry to tell you that your services will not be needed any more this season." I was astonished, and I asked Mr Wostinholm what it all meant. He answered that my play had not been satisfactory. When I pressed him to explain, he said, "You have had a glass too much." I denied the charge, but it was all no use … I went then to the hotel where I usually put up and was seen by a number of persons who were highly indignant at the treatment I had received, and whom I can call to prove that I was perfectly sober.'

However, A.A. Thomson in his book *Hirst and Rhodes*, told how George Hirst had related Peel had emerged on the day of the incident 'in a proper condition' and he had been persuaded to go back to bed to sleep it off. Hirst got to the ground and explained to Hawke that Peel had been taken ill in the night only for Peel to stagger on to the pitch just before play started 'in an even properer condition'. The exact circumstances surrounding Peel's dramatic downfall will forever be doubted. For what it's worth I find online historian 'Old Ebor' plausible. He too doubts the urinating on the pitch story and believes that someone related that Peel was sacked for being 'pissed at the wicket' which has been widely expanded to 'pissed on the wicket'.

Peel did achieve what Peate never did – play in a Championship-winning Yorkshire side. He was an integral part of the team which won the title in 1893 and 1896. When Peate was in his pomp, Peel was very much in his shadow, operating more as a batsman who could bowl a bit. Even in Peate's final season, 1886, when he took 'only' 68 wickets at 13.42, Peel could hardly be considered a bowling rival, taking 27 at 21.96. But once Peate was out of the way, Peel's bowling figures soared. He took 98 in the first year of Peate's absence, 1887 (R.S. Holmes' figures), and for the next nine seasons topped 100 wickets in a season. It shows remarkable acuity by Hawke to have realised that by shunting Peate aside, he would be gaining runs without serious detriment to wickets taken.

The way Lord Hawke indulged Peel begs the question why did he come down so harshly on Peate? The stories of Peel's drinking exploits are legion, Peate's less so. Why did he tolerate only a couple of seasons of Peate when his position as Yorkshire supremo was still open to challenge yet happily pick Peel time after time when his authority at Yorkshire was unassailable? It adds further credence to the likelihood that Hawke knew Peel was the future, Peate would be the past. In a first-class career Peel bowled 88,163 balls, taking 1,775 wickets at an average of 16.20 with best figures of 9-22. By comparison Peate bowled 47,025 balls and took 1,076 wickets at an average of 13.49 with best figures of 8-5. Peate's batting average was 10.64, Peel's 19.44.

Whether it was form or discipline which brought about Peate's end, losing a place in the county team was potentially catastrophic for any professional cricketer. For some, roles such as coaching, umpiring or working on a ground staff offered one potential escape route. Peate at least had his shop and his exploits for both Yorkshire and England would have provided the celebrity factor. However, his income would have been affected and for the next 13 years until his death in 1900 he struggled to keep his head above water. Reports from the time declare that his family was destitute at the time of his death.

Peate's colleague and friend, Tom Emmett, was another to receive a benefit. In his autobiography Hawke says that Emmett received £620, a sum which a successful provincial lawyer or architect would have been delighted to receive as an annual salary. Among others to receive a benefit from the county were John Thewlis, George Pinder, Ephraim Lockwood, Allen Hill, Billy Bates, Louis Hall and Bobby Peel. Peate's contribution to Yorkshire stands up well alongside those but his departure from the Yorkshire side in his eighth season was to prove financially damaging. Yorkshire's rule on ten seasons for a benefit was rigid.

Despite Lord Hawke's inflexible 'rules are rules' stance regarding Peate's benefit, he did have a sympathetic attitude to professionals. As we have seen, he was fond of, and indulgent of, characters such as Emmett and Peel and Hawke drove through reforms which improved the economic position of the professionals. One of them was a minimum guaranteed £1,000 should any professional be awarded a benefit with the proviso that two-thirds would be held back for the player's wife and children rather than being handed directly to the player and risk it being wasted on drink.

Another innovation brought in by Hawke which benefited the Yorkshire professionals was winter pay. Introduced from 7 September 1896, each professional received £2 per week. Not a fortune, but similar to what a man might have expected to have earned in the mills. Winter pay was seen as very much Hawke's initiative and it cemented the loyalty of the professionals. In an interview with *Cricket* magazine he explained his views: 'One has to consider that men while playing cricket have very little opportunity for saving; you expect them to work hard for you all the summer and then cast them off to get whatever work they can. It has often been said to me that men are all the better for working during the winter but apart from the fact that they cannot always get work, I don't believe in men going into hot mills for the winter.' This was, of course, exactly what Ted Peate had to contend with, but Hawke's innovations came too late for him.

Chapter 9

Decline and Fall

ON 1 April 1889, magistrates sitting in Otley approved the transfer of the licence of the White Swan pub in Yeadon to Edmund Peate. For many professional sportsmen of his day, a life running a pub was an attractive proposition, celebrity status helping to draw in the customers. Peate's career for his county and his country were only just behind him so his name was still a big drawing card. The sports outfitters shop in central Leeds was proving successful and he was picking up match fees turning out for his local cricket club. Now he was in charge of his own pub. The White Swan was a large venue which doubled up as a clubhouse for Peate's beloved Yeadon Cricket Club. It had a large room which was also used as a viewing gallery for the on-field activities (it still does today) and was big enough to host functions, notably the annual dinner of the cricket club. Although owned by Hammonds Brewery, Peate should have been the ideal tenant whose fame would increase the pub's takings. The downside was the temptation of readily available alcohol. Many a sportsman found the pub trade the start of a downward spiral. However, less than 12 months later, Peate had given up the licence as the same magistrates transferred it to a David Birch. It was not the close proximity to alcohol which was behind the decision to give up the White Swan so quickly, he was going because he had received the offer of another lucrative appointment – and from an unexpected source.

On 11 October of 1889 the *Wharfedale Observer* announced that Peate had been engaged as manager and head professional of the newly formed Leeds Cricket, Football and Athletic Club. The new enterprise had secured significant land from the estate of Lord Cardigan which it was to develop into Headingley stadium and cricket ground. 'The berth is a good one and Peate commences his duties on Monday, the laying out of the ground having to be superintended,' said the report. Intriguingly, it said he had beaten George Ulyett and Saul Wade in securing the post. A new cricket team calling itself simply Leeds would be formed (chiefly from the Leeds Clarendon Club) to play on the ground under the captaincy of Samuel R Jackson, a wealthy Leeds hat manufacturer, who would go on to develop a warm relationship with Peate throughout the decade. In 1900 Jackson had eight hat shops in Leeds and a hat-making factory at Mabgate in the Burmantofts area of the city. While Jackson was the captain of the new club, significantly the chairman and driving force behind it was Lord Hawke, and it is impossible to imagine that if he had sacked Peate because of his ill discipline and drinking habits he would then have sanctioned his appointment to this key role just a couple of years later. It is inconceivable that a man with Hawke's reputation was showing pangs of guilt about his decision to terminate Peate's Yorkshire career and the appointment was surely on merit – and, if the *Wharfedale Observer* was correct, beating off the likes of Ulyett and Wade, whose Yorkshire careers were still very much alive. Peate's role was not just as playing professional for the new Leeds club but also as manager of the Headingley complex.

At this stage there was no suggestion that Peate's playing career with Yeadon would be severed. In November 1889 he and Mrs Peate served up 'an excellent repast' for Yeadon CC's annual dinner in the White Swan and then collected the club bowling prize (86 wickets, average 6.98). But in January 1890 Peate announced that he was leaving not just the cricket club but the pub and indeed the town itself and moving to Headingley. Peate's farewell was treated locally as a minor disaster. The *Wharfedale Observer* commented on 24 January 1890: 'This severance of old ties will be a matter of deep regret to all Yeadoners for there is no doubt that all the town has looked upon Ted as its own special property. Wherever he went, whether to a local cricket match or to the Antipodes, his career was watched with an all-absorbing interest and the champion Yorkshire bowler was half-worshipped by all who handled a bat or trundled the leather. So his departure for another scene of action is regarded as a public calamity.'

So highly regarded was Peate that a testimonial was announced to mark his achievements at Yeadon. The *Wharfedale Observer* waxed (on 7 February): 'Ted, my boy, you will see whether the people of Yeadon appreciate you or not! We venture to say that the result will prove that though they are sorry to part with you, even if it is for your good, they will not allow you to leave "Good Old Yeadon" without a substantial token of their respect and esteem.' The secretary of Yeadon CC was charged with organising the printing of subscription sheets (pledges to donate to the fund) and placing them in public places.

The testimonial fund from his erstwhile Yeadon colleagues rumbled on through the summer and the presentation took place in late October 1890 at the pub where Peate had briefly held the licence, the White Swan – or rather it didn't. The *Wharfedale Observer* reported that it had been intended to present Peate with an 'illuminated address' but it could not be got ready in time and would therefore be handed to him on a future date. An illuminated address was a framed scroll, written by a calligrapher and usually on calfskin vellum, often with an embroidered ribbon or seal, and which extolled the virtues of the beneficiary. Evidently there was some cash left over as later reports stated that he was also recipient of two armchairs from this fund. The *Observer*'s report is useful in that it tabulates Peate's career achievements for Yeadon. Despite his first-class career, he had still managed to appear at least once for Yeadon every season between 1877 and 1890. Once Yorkshire had dispensed with his services, these appearances were more frequent and his bowling figures showed no sign of a diminution of his powers. His most prolific season had been 1888 when he took 112 wickets, average 5.76.

Mr Thompson Marshall gave a toast to his future and said Peate had shed lustre on the village of Yeadon and his loss had been keenly felt on the pitch that summer but he would provide an inspiration to the coming generation. After drinking their toast, the audience burst into song with 'For he's a jolly good fellow'. There then followed a rare record of Peate giving a speech and he was critical of the way Yeadon players practised. Coming from a player who had been given the tainted reputation of being somewhat lax in his habits, this might seem a bit rich. The report reads:

'Peate said he thanked them very much for the enthusiastic manner in which they had drunk his health. He was very sorry that the record of Yeadon was so very, very bad as it was in the past season. He thought he could explain one cause of it, and that was the mode of practice which was carried on (Hear, hear). He called it a terribly rotten system but, on the other hand, he really had no remedy except the players themselves. At present, when practising, they batted five minutes if they were bowled out before the expiration of that time and ten minutes if they could hold on by hook or by crook. He called that a terribly rotten system. The players did not go in to practise as if they were in a match (Hear, hear). They simply got hold of the bat; it was Tom, Jack or Bill bowling and he said "Oh, can I ball thee aght." "Nay tha cannot" and the sole idea was to keep the ball off the wickets for the specified ten minutes. There was no regard to playing in a proper and scientific manner; the ball was hit straight up and the result was that when the players went into a match they acted in a similar manner and were soon out. He would recommend both old and young players of the club to practise in the same spirit as they would play in a match and do their utmost to get the ball away, keep it down and keep it off the wickets. If this were done the result would be that the players would have better averages, the club would have a better record and there would be more renown to the players all round.' With that Peate thanked them again and sat down. The illuminated address arrived later.

On 27 May 1890 the Headingley ground staged its first ever cricket match, Leeds taking on Scarborough. The match drew a crowd of a little under 5,000 and although the ground was clearly unfinished with building work still going on, the *Yorkshire Post* was convinced it would become the 'most complete centre of athletic competitions in the North of England'. As well as hosting the cricket square there was a football field to be used by what would become Leeds Rugby League Football Club, a running track and tennis courts. Peate's friend S.R. Jackson opened the batting for Leeds and made 43 runs as the players were joined by around 30 invited guests for lunch. The speaker was wealthy businessman George Bray, who had made his fortune in gas lighting mantles and had poured a large sum into the Headingley venture, and he confirmed that an official opening would be held later. Alas for the new club, their first game at the ground ended in an eight-wicket defeat. Peate took eight wickets in the match and, despite coming in as last man, top scored with 20 in the Leeds second innings of only 106. There was better news when Haslingden visited and were beaten on 30 May.

Peate was very much the mainstay of the Leeds team and his wickets helped Leeds to wins over the likes of Bradford and Sheffield, so when a fixture between the North of England and the Australian tourists was arranged at Headingley for 1 September 1890, form, history and the attraction of the home club's star player was enough to earn him selection for the North. *Cricket* magazine described it as the first match of real importance at Headingley and was full of praise for the ground. Alas it was not a very strong North side as Yorkshire and Nottinghamshire players were involved in important fixtures, although it did include a 20-year-old F.S. Jackson, the future Yorkshire captain and president. The Australians were considered a pale imitation of previous tourists and they lost more matches than they won on this tour. Even so, the North were well beaten and Peate was only entrusted with 19 overs across two innings with the North relying on Lancashire and England's Johnny Briggs and Leicestershire's Dick Pougher. In the first innings the North were skittled out for 75 and their second-top scorer was none other than Peate, with 13, despite it being a long time since his last first-class appearance. However, no-one came to watch Peate with a bat in his hand and his bowling was hardly scintillating.

For the Leeds club, it was a different story and Peate's figures of 117 wickets at an average of 8.30 were good enough to earn him a second contract at Headingley and it seems as though he was required to get involved in coaching as well. The Leeds club were running two teams and for the start of the 1891 season, the *Yorkshire Post* noted that there were 93 ordinary matches and three county matches organised for the ground that year. Peate was retained 'in order to teach the rising talent how to bat and bowl' along with Bent, Harris and Hayley. Hayley, who made seven appearances for Yorkshire, was to recur in Peate's history at a later date while Harris was possibly William Harris, who had four matches for the county.

The future looked bright for Peate but suddenly it all fell apart. On 4 August 1891, the *Yorkshire Post* ran a short advertisement: 'E Peate. Open for matches for rest of season. Apply 44 North Lane, Headingley.' Leeds no longer required his services. He was still performing well for Leeds so what had happened? If Peate had fallen out with the powers that be at Leeds, it must have been something serious for them to terminate his employment so suddenly. Had Lord Hawke once again come to the conclusion that Peate was incorrigible and far from being a reformed character, his behaviour was unacceptable? Maddeningly, the sources are all quiet. The best clue we have is the comment at the club's annual meeting held on 9 October 1891 by the chairman W.B. Nicholson who said that 'he was sorry to lose the services of two of their professionals namely Harris and Peate' but shed no further light on their departure. The club did announce that they were to cut back to just three professionals for 1892 and welcomed the arrival of Taylor, who had been a professional with Castleford and Hunslet but was hardly in Peate's class.

All this tends to point to a cost-cutting rather than a disciplinary measure. Peate would have demanded a premium for his services based on his past reputation which theoretically would have brought more spectators through the turnstiles. However, he also had responsibilities as a groundsman and there is no record of him having any experience in the role. Nicholson also said in his report to the AGM that he thought from a financial perspective that the club had played too many matches in midweek and next season Leeds would concentrate on 'good local matches on Saturdays and visits from clubs of national repute in midweek'. Peate's performances on the pitch cannot have been a reason behind the decision. He had taken 154 wickets at a cost of 1,416 runs, second only to Hayley's 173 for 1,549 but this was despite Peate not appearing for Leeds throughout August.

So, in August 1891, Peate was touting for business and played five one-off matches as a professional. He turned out twice for Hovingham and once for Armley, North Leeds and Ripon, this latter appearance ironically against his old employers Leeds. Curiously, there is virtually no reporting on the match in the newspapers of the time, the Leeds-based *Yorkshire Evening Post*, which came out on the afternoon of the opening day stating simply that Ripon had secured the services of E Peate and he had taken three early wickets.

The season of 1892 was a difficult one for Peate. He was uncommitted to any club, turning out for whoever would pay him the most, trading on his name and reputation. He was still a big draw and in August 1893 Peate agreed terms to join an invitational team called Yorkshire Wanderers on a tour to Holland. He played a total of six matches, the final one being a match against an All Holland XI. The Dutch were preparing for a tour of England the following season and were keen to get some experience. Peate was the only professional in the Wanderers side which also included his former captain at Leeds S.R. Jackson, the wealthy hat manufacturer who was a keen and decent amateur (he even managed one first-class game for Yorkshire, against Lancashire at Old Trafford – if you are only going to play one game there can be no better opponents). Another ex-county man, Harry Leadbetter, who played six games for Yorkshire between 1884 and 1890 (all of them against MCC) was in the party. The Dutch found Peate unplayable as he took 9-20. The Dutch were much improved in their second innings, Peate only taking the one wicket but it may be that the Wanderers were keen not to humiliate their inexperienced opponents and were holding back. The full bowling figures for the game are lost. A photograph exists of the two teams lined up with Peate in the centre. Now approaching 40 years of age, he does not look in any way overweight, a full head of hair accompanying his familiar drooping moustache and a confident look at the camera. Overall, he took 64 wickets in the six games, at an average of just over 4.

A *Yorkshire Post* article appearing a fortnight after their return was clearly based on an interview with one of the touring party and reveals that all the matches were played on coconut matting. 'The English bowlers found this artificial carpet fast and true and were not surprised to find that the Dutchmen had been accustomed to quick bowling,' said the article. 'There were so few spectators, in spite of sensational and unlimited advertising, that on many occasions half the gate money would have amounted to a few coppers only for each player. It is surprising that under these conditions good cricket should be played by Dutch teams ... Indeed, the results would have been much less favourable to the visitors than they were if the Dutchmen had not been profoundly puzzled by the slow bowling of Peate. It is said that this bowler, in the days of his early achievements, used to practise break-bowling all through the winter on the wooden floor of a warehouse and so the cocoa-nut matting offered no difficulty to him. But the Dutchmen had never seen bowling so deliberate and so illusory.'

A few days after returning from Holland, Peate was turning out in a benefit match for Jim Yeadon. Confusingly Yeadon was actually born in Yeadon and turned out for his home town club. He played three times for Yorkshire in 1888. He scored 41 runs across six innings with a high score of 22 (average 10.25) and made three stumpings. His duties at Yeadon included groundsman, like so many other club professionals, but he met with a terrible accident in 1893 when he fell between the shafts of the heavy roller while tending to the ground and broke both his legs. 'The unfortunate accident has, of course, deprived the poor fellow of a means of gaining a livelihood and with the object of affording him some assistance, the club with which he gained his training has started a subscription on his behalf,' said the *Wharfedale Observer*. The match was played on Wednesday, 23 August 1893 between Yeadon and Peate's XI, which significantly included Stephen Doughty, the resident professional at Skipton who carried out similar ground duties to Jim Yeadon. The game was played during the Yeadon and Guiseley holiday week, when all the town's mills and factories were closed and a gala was held on the cricket field at the weekend. Unfortunately for Yeadon (the player), 1893 was a depressed year for the textile industry and most factories were on short time working, driving down income. To make it worse, the weather was not good and this combination produced a sparse attendance. The receipts from the game were only just over £10 and Yeadon would have to rely on appeals to boost his fund. As for the cricket, Peate was wicketless (if he did any bowling) with his Skipton acquaintance Doughty taking seven Yeadon wickets in their total of 121. It was a curious game – Peate's team lost wickets quickly and Peate came in to bat last and scored 26 not out while at the other end Doughty was 44 not out. However, they were still 20 short of victory (or from the Yeadon club point of view, one wicket from defeat) when stumps were drawn at 6pm and the match was declared a draw, despite the cries of 'play it out' from disappointed spectators.

Peate's glorious performances for county and country were now an increasingly distant memory, albeit one which cropped up regularly in magazine and newspaper articles about the past featuring reminiscences by former cricketers. One such interview was with Australian captain Billy Murdoch, who had no hesitation in naming Peate as the best bowler he had ever faced. He said there were many contenders for the best batsman, but Peate was unrivalled for his bowling.

Peate still had his supporters across the game. Rev. R.S. Holmes wrote a weekly (and lengthy) article for *Cricket* magazine. In June 1894 he wondered why Peate and Nottinghamshire's Alfred Shaw had been dropped so hastily by their respective counties. Holmes, who was to write a definitive history of Yorkshire ten years later, commented: 'I am by no means certain that Peate is not still the best bowler in Yorkshire, in spite of his ample girth and defective eyesight which now requires the help of glasses.' Holmes, a Methodist minister and respected cricket historian, returned to the subject just three editions later on 12 July, writing: 'Here in Yorkshire we have a team called the Skipton CC; hitherto very third rate. They engage Peate to bowl in their matches and at once they become first class.' This dismissal of Skipton as third rate was to annoy Skipton sufficiently that the secretary was instructed to write to the magazine refuting their comments about the club. Their letter was not printed and any reply was lost.

Holmes was clearly one of Peate's staunchest supporters and the 18 April 1895 edition of *Cricket* once again champions the Peate cause. The article relates that Peate had turned out for the Leeds Barbers XI against J.T. Penrose's XI in an early-season game. This possibly was not a professional engagement but Holmes states: 'The barbers engaged the services of a grand old bowler, almost as good as any yet in the county of broad acres – the ex-county player Peate. He took the whole of the eleven wickets, at what cost was not stated, but as the total from the bat was only fifty, twenty, I should say, would be a fairly accurate guess. I have occasionally seen Peate bowl during the past five years and have heard more of his doings and one cannot but regret his early retirement from front rank cricket. A thousand pities both for himself and for cricket. By his bowling he has recently changed a third class club into a first class one.' (The Skipton reference again.) In fact this game was a charity match played for the benefit of non-union employees in the shoe industry who were caught out in a national trades dispute. The union was seeking a minimum wage of 30 shillings (£1.50) a week and in response the Federation of Shoe Manufacturers locked out all workers in a dispute which lasted six weeks. While union men received some small pay, those not in a union were left on their own and Peate's agreement to play in this game (presumably for free) indicates sympathy for the cause, particularly given Peate's own distinctly working-class background. His membership of Guiseley Conservative Club and election as one of numerous club vice-presidents does not necessarily mean he had Conservative sympathies.

In April 1894 Peate was still offering his services on a precarious match-by-match basis. He was reunited with former colleagues Ulyett and Peel alongside Yorkshire first-teamer Arthur Sellers to play for a side run by a wealthy Leeds businessman, R.S. Kirk. For his 30th birthday on 22 April the cricket-mad Kirk had arranged a game for his team called Leeds Buckingham against Yorkshire Relish at the Armley club's ground in Leeds. Kirk lived at Buckingham Villas (later home of Leeds Girls' School and now a special educational needs centre called West Oaks) which was just round the corner from Peate's home. It cannot be said that Kirk was simply doing his neighbour a favour as Peate was still a formidable bowler. He made his point and took seven wickets for Buckingham while his replacement in the Yorkshire team, Bobby Peel, took three. Of course, the calibre of the opposition is not known. Yorkshire Relish was the highest-selling bottled sauce in the Victorian era and was produced at a factory in Leeds, so their team was almost certainly backed by another cricket loving factory owner. They were good enough to get Ulyett and Bates out for a combined 25 and restricted Kirk's team to a total of 93 (Kirk came in as last man and was run out for a duck) with Peel making an unbeaten 43. The Relish side lost the challenge game by 42 runs.

Peate continued to offer his services via regular advertisements in the *Yorkshire Post* and when the 1894 season started he played for Barnsley and his old club Yeadon. But then in stepped an ambitious club from the further reaches of the West Riding. Skipton was to provide Peate with regular (but not exclusive) employment for the next six seasons. Skipton had previous experience of Peate's effectiveness at club level. In July 1889 Skipton had hosted a touring side called N.R. Hepworth's XI based mainly on the Leeds Clarendon team – Clarendon was the club which a year later was to become the Leeds CC based at Headingley – and Peate was engaged to play for the visitors. The local paper, the *Craven Herald*, reported: 'Peate was simply unplayable and the Skipton batsmen fell as many hundreds have done before.' He took eight wickets in seven overs for ten runs as Skipton were all out for 35 chasing Clarendon's 115. To avoid disappointing the crowd, the Skipton side were asked to bat again, this time with Peate playing no part in the attack. Without him they reached 56/4. Stephen Doughty, the long-time Skipton professional (and the same man who was to play alongside Peate in the charity match for Jim Yeadon), fell to the second ball of the day bowled by Peate.

This feat must have been firmly in the minds of the Skipton committee when they met at the Ship Hotel in

Skipton in March 1893. They were about to enter the newly formed West Yorkshire League and reckoned they needed a star name to not only draw in the crowds but also give them a fighting chance. The club's president was the Duke of Devonshire, whose extensive Yorkshire estates came right up to the boundaries of the town, and it was bankrolled by the Dewhurst family, whose Skipton mill was the world's largest producer of cotton sewing thread, every week churning out a million small bobbins of thread in 300 different colours. Ironically, however, the family were devoted Congregationalists and the patriarch of the family was a pillar of the local temperance movement. Despite this, Peate's alleged drinking does not appear to have been an issue for Skipton. The committee resolved 'that additional professional assistance be obtained in the following matches: Keighley, Bradford, Bowling Old Lane, Bingley, Bowling Old Lane, Bradford, Keighley and that the above dates be offered to E. Peate and H. Beaumont'.

In 1893 Peate was employed by Skipton on an ad hoc basis (he missed much of August due to the tour of Holland) but in 1894 the committee offered, and he accepted, a deal to play in all Skipton's league fixtures, leaving him free to take up other engagements to boost his income when Skipton held a non-league fixture. Skipton already engaged Stephen Doughty, who had had a modest career with Derbyshire as the club's ground professional – required to open and close the ground and tend to the surface. The addition of Peate strengthened the team immeasurably and guaranteed the player regular income throughout the summer at last.

Skipton's bold move provided an instant return. Peate topped the bowling average list in the league's first season taking 40 wickets at a cost of 313 runs, an average of 7.83. Only one player took more wickets (44) and that was a name from Peate's Yorkshire past – George 'Shoey' Harrison, who had appeared on the county scene so spectacularly only to suffer a dislocated shoulder which greatly reduced his effectiveness in later years. Harrison turned out for Bowling Old Lane, who finished next to bottom of the seven-team league. Skipton would have been pleased to finish third in the table, which allocated one point for a win, minus one point for a loss and nothing for a draw. Bradford topped the league with six points while Skipton finished with three (five wins and two losses). Occasionally Peate would come across some of his erstwhile Yorkshire colleagues who were turning out for clubs in the league when Yorkshire were not playing. For example, on 1 May 1897, the Skipton team travelled to Dewsbury for the first match of that season. The home side featured the man who had first been Peate's junior colleague but then replaced him in the Yorkshire side, Bobby Peel. It was an easy win for Dewsbury, who reduced Skipton to 36 all out with Peel bowling Peate for a duck. Both men took three wickets in the match.

* * *

As well as his shop, Peate continued to seek paid cricketing opportunities wherever offered. In 1895, however, one potentially lucrative venture was closed. John Thomas North, a fabulously wealthy businessman, hired Peate to put together a side to bring down to his mansion at Eltham in London to play against his team drawn from the locality. North was a colourful character. Born in Leeds as the son of a coal merchant, he emigrated to South America for greater opportunities in his line of engineering. While there he began building up an empire in railways, iron and coal fields and the export of vast quantities of guano – essentially seabird droppings – which were exported back to Europe for use as fertiliser. He had well-placed connections in the Chilean government (which may well have been secured by bribery) and which protected his monopolies. In England he built a mansion set in 600 acres in Avery Hill, Eltham, which is now a teacher training college. North never forgot his Leeds roots. He bought the ruins of Kirkstall Abbey on the banks of the river Aire for £10,000 and promptly gave it to the city of Leeds. He also made significant donations to the Leeds Infirmary and what would become Leeds University. He was better known to the Victorian public as 'Colonel North', a purely honorary title bestowed because he regularly allowed his grounds to be used by the Tower Hamlets Regiment of Volunteers (a forerunner of the Territorial Army) because of its specialism in engineering. Peate must have been delighted when the Colonel appointed him to put together a team. The *Yorkshire Post* of 6 August 1895 reported that Peate had received many applications for places in the team and the task of selecting those who wanted to play would not have been easy. However, the Colonel called the match off because his wife became ill and he chose to spend the rest of the summer at the German spa town of Bad Homburg, a favourite destination of European ancestry, including Kaiser Wilhelm of Germany. The following year North was dead and so the lucrative project for Peate was lost.

Back in Yorkshire, Peate was continuing to play for Skipton in the West Yorkshire League with much success. On 24 August 1895 he took 9-17 as Skipton bowled out Manningham for 38. He was also continuing to pick up games elsewhere. On Wednesday, 15 July, between his Skipton engagements, his old club Leeds selected him to play in an away match at Dalton-in-Furness, Cumbria. He pops up in the end of season averages published in local newspapers having had one game for the likes of Yeadon and Leeds Buckingham. On 8 August 1888 he linked up with his old mate Tom Emmett to travel to Llwynypia in the Rhondda Valley to play for the club side against the Glamorgan county XI. It was a one-day match so presumably the pair were well rewarded for travelling such a long distance. Glamorgan were then a minor county side and the locals must have regretted the expense when Emmett was out for 2 and Peate, batting at number three, for a duck. Llwynypia made 67 and it may be a reflection of the state of the pitch when Emmett and Peate redeemed themselves by skittling out Glamorgan for just 20. Peate took five wickets, Emmett two, there were two run-outs and one player did not take the field. Glamorgan were invited to bat again and this time made 61, with Peate taking eight wickets and Emmett two as Llwynypia recorded an eight-wicket win. Presumably the Welshmen were content.

An interesting court case arose in 1897 which hints at the bad reputation some of the older Yorkshire cricketers had at this point. The case took place at the Leeds City Police Court and was reported in the *Yorkshire Post* on 9 November 1897. The report is quoted in full: 'Albert Percy Charlesworth (32) of 42 Scotchman Lane, Morley, the well-known Hull and Yorkshire County professional cricketer and Mary Taylor (33), a married woman, of 9 Plevna Grove, Hunslet, were charged with having committed an offence in Assembly Street, Leeds. The case excited considerable interest among cricketers in the district and in the court were seen R. Peel, E. Peate and W. Middlebrook, all ex-members of the Yorkshire County team. After evidence had been given by Detective Bowman and Police Constable Haigh, Mr Arthur Willey, for the defence, pointed out several discrepancies in their statements and totally denied the allegation of misconduct. Witnesses having spoken to the higher character of both defendants, the magistrates held that the evidence of the police was not strong enough to secure a conviction and dismissed the charge.'

The report is infuriatingly short of information. What was the charge? Why was there emphasis on the fact that Mary Taylor was a 'married woman'? Was it poor journalism that left so many questions unanswered or a decision to offer a little more latitude to a well-known sportsman than to a working man? In the absence of the salient details, one has to draw conclusions. The incident happened in the street. The police considered it serious enough to bring the case in front of the magistrates when people of some standing in the community might under normal circumstances have been escorted home without creating a fuss if there was some suspicion of intoxication. And, of course, there is that emphasis on the 'married woman'. We do not know if she and Charlesworth were together or if the two had some sort of altercation. We are also left with the suspicion that the background to the case was well known to those in cricketing circles, where it caused 'great excitement'. Charlesworth (who played just seven matches for Yorkshire between 1894 and 1895) was supported in court by Peel and Peate, two famous international sportsmen and Middlebrook, of lesser fame but who had 17 Yorkshire appearances under his belt.

The timing of this case may also have been of significance. Peel had been sacked by Yorkshire, or rather Lord Hawke, a few weeks previously for drunkenness. As related in the previous chapter, stories emerged that he had urinated on the pitch in the match against Middlesex in Sheffield in July, allegations disputed as an embellishment by plenty of cricket historians. However, it seems indisputable that he was unable to take to the field on the morning of the third day's play due to his heavy drinking and was slurring and unsteady on his feet when he did appear. Peel was later to say '[Lord Hawke] put his arm around me and escorted me off the field and out of Yorkshire cricket. What a gentleman.' This comment has been described as either highly gracious or highly sarcastic.

Hawke, for his part, wrote that sacking Peel was the most decisive action of his entire career. 'It had to be done for the sake of discipline and for the good of cricket. Nothing ever gave me so much pain.' He went on to write that Peel was thoroughly loyal and 'emphasise how admirably he has since made good'. However, in his autobiography of Lord Hawke, James Coldham said that 'when he declared "nothing ever gave me so much pain" the sceptics were unconvinced, no doubt remembering Edmund Peate'. We are left with the impression that this court case was the result of a boys' night out gone wrong. Peel and Peate were known to enjoy a drink, and Middlebrook and Charlesworth were in their circle. Neither of the latter two merit a mention in Lord Hawke's lengthy memoirs.

Meanwhile, Peate's career was meandering towards a close. His annual contract with Skipton was reliable enough but the invitations from other clubs were becoming sparse. Now past 40, 1897 was also the year that the interview with the maestro, referred to in previous chapters, appeared in the *Yorkshire Evening Post* under the byline 'Old Ebor', alias Alfred Pullin, which was to be collated into a book, *Talks With Old English Cricketers*, published in 1900. The newspaper article is accompanied by a sketch of Peate. The contrast between the drawing and the photograph of the team in Holland only four years previously is striking. Peate is noticeably older and the artist makes no attempt to hide the fact that he has put on a lot of weight. His walrus moustache is firmly in place but now the eyes are behind a pair of circular spectacles which he needed to get through his appearances.

However, on the pitch, Peate was still performing for Skipton. In 1898 he took 73 wickets at an average of 10.52 as Skipton finished joint top of the West Yorkshire League only to be well beaten in a play-off with Bradford for the trophy. But, off the field, the cost of playing in the West Yorkshire League was taking its toll. Skipton were so poorly supported that they tried to boost their income by trying an athletics meeting, offering good prizes across a wide range of challenges and handicap races. These types of events could bring in the crowds and turn a profit. However, it rained and the event made a loss. The West Riding League now included fixtures against teams like Barnsley and Wakefield and travelling costs were mounting. Peate's services did not come cheaply. In 1895 Skipton reported a loss of £36 which increased to £43 the following year and £42 in 1897. Skipton's remorseless battle to stay solvent prompted the 'Notes and Queries' column of the *Craven Herald* to observe that 'Instead of dribbling by in dozens they [the public] should consider the first-class cricket they can witness, attend in their hundreds and thus maintain, untrammelled by the depressive effects of debt, a club whose performances are a credit to the town.' In 1901 the club's total gate receipts for the season were just £21, a figure described by the club secretary William Farey as 'a disgrace to the town'. That year the club was saved from bankruptcy when its captain, Edgar Dewhurst, returned from the Boer War, walked into the bank and wrote out a cheque for £130 to pay off all the club's outstanding debts. However, in his absence, cost-cutting measures had been taken and one of the major victims was Peate.

Skipton were not alone in finding the costs of the West Yorkshire League onerous and in 1899 the competition was scrapped. This was Peate's final season and on the field his performances held up. True, he was now barely able to run at more than an amble due to his weight and age. His eyesight was poor leading to dropped catches but in his last season he again topped the Skipton bowling averages with 60 wickets. His average had sneaked up to 12.68. The axe was not far off. Skipton had not just Peate as its professional but also the old stalwart Stephen Doughty. Although much inferior as a player, Doughty was also the club groundsman and was a diligent and reliable employee who had been at Skipton for more than 15 years. At the final committee meeting of the season the officials resolved that only one professional could be hired for the 1900 season. There, in just a few words of a committee resolution, the cricket career of Ted Peate was closed.

The future for Ted Peate was fairly bleak. There could not be too many more paydays squeezed out of his fading body and, unlike some of his contemporaries such as Louis Hall, he had not plotted a route into a coaching role. The shop in central Leeds was long established but the evidence is that profits were diminishing. Certainly there was more than just Peate and Ephraim Lockwood advertising in the newspapers. All around him, his world seemed to be falling away. His great pal from his Yorkshire days George Ulyett was in poor health. His final county game was in 1893 and after watching Yorkshire in action at Sheffield he contracted pneumonia and died on 18 June 1898. Just after Christmas 1899 a Yorkshire stalwart from the past, John Thewlis, died and Peate's spin bowling partner Billy Bates got off his sickbed to attend his funeral. Bates died of pneumonia on 8 January 1900.

A few weeks later, on Monday, 5 March 1900, possibly to celebrate his birthday on 2 March, Peate went to the Grand Theatre in Leeds to see the D'Oyly Carte light opera company's opening night performance of Gilbert and Sullivan's *The Mikado*. There was a cold northerly wind and the occasional heavy shower that day and when Peate woke the next morning at his home, 15 St Michael's Road, Headingley, he was feeling unwell and confined to his bed. At first there was no concern and his old captain at Leeds and good friend S.R. Jackson visited him twice on the Wednesday. Some reports described this illness as a congested liver, which is when the liver becomes 'waterlogged' as a result of back pressure from a heart that is ceasing to pump efficiently. There are many reasons why the heart might not function properly although excess alcohol could be one. Peate was described as 'restive' and got up after Jackson's visit. His condition quickly became more serious, and pneumonia developed on the Thursday. He died on the Sunday morning at 5.15am.

The funeral took place just two days later, on the afternoon of Tuesday, 13 March. Peate's coffin, bearing the inscription 'Edmund Peate died March 11 1900 aged 44 years', was taken from his house and loaded on to a horse-drawn hearse. From there the funeral cortege made its way to Yeadon, a journey of more than six miles, where a large assembly had gathered at his old pub and Yeadon CC headquarters, the White Swan. From there it was carried by Skipton club representatives to the Yeadon cemetery along a route lined by residents out to pay their respects. The service was conducted by the Yeadon vicar, Rev. D.F. Bradley, and wreaths were laid on behalf of the Skipton, Leeds and Leeds Buckingham cricket clubs, R.S. Kirk, W. Farey, S.R. Jackson, Mr H. Daniel and Miss Kent. The identity of the latter two is not known[1]. The *Wharfedale Observer* noted that he was buried very close to his great friend Thomas Blatchley, an enthusiastic member of the Yeadon club who ran a chemist's shop in the town. It was Thomas Blatchley who was the recipient of the letter from Australia published in his local paper which is quoted in chapter four.

---

1   The 1900 Robinson's Leeds street directory lists a Mary Kent of Woodhouse Lane, Leeds, as a confectioner and 'Misses' Kent of Woodhouse Street, Leeds, also as confectioners. The year after Ted's death, his widow was running a confectioner's shop (see page 214). It is possible that Sarah Peate was working at one of the Kent shops and saw this as a way to make a living after her husband's death.

There were several playing members and dignitaries from the Yeadon, Skipton and Leeds clubs and a representative from each of the following clubs: Armley, North Leeds, Pudsey St Pauls, Stourton, Dewsbury, Farsley, Horsforth Hall Park, Guiseley and Colne. Sadly, the only colleague from Peate's old Yorkshire days was George Harrison. In fairness, Tom Emmett had moved to Leicester while Bobby Peel was coaching in Essex while Ulyett and Bates were dead. The whereabouts of Lord Hawke are not known and there is no record of any wreath or message on behalf of the county cricket club. There were two Yorkshire area committee members, although as they were recorded as representing their clubs, Leeds and Skipton, it seems a rather mean-spirited response. The *Wharfedale Observer* thought so. It said: 'Also present in a private capacity were Mr J.W. Bannister of Leeds and Mr F. Thornton of Skipton, both members of the Yorkshire County Committee but it was a matter of regret that neither the Yorkshire County Club nor the Yorkshire cricket eleven were directly represented at the funeral of one who in his day had done not a little to uphold his county's reputation. Whatever his faults, he was at least deserving of that measure of respect from those who profited by his powers.'

The papers paid tribute to his prowess and recounted his exploits both for his county and his country. The *Wharfedale Observer* said he was one of, if not the best slow bowler the game had ever seen. It described him as 'the most genial of cricketers' and said he was 'a general favourite with all classes of the community'. Skipton's paper, the *Craven Herald*, hinted that Peate had enjoyed the social aspects of the game in its tribute: 'Whether it was during a lull in the game or an after-dinner speech at the Ship Hotel, he was equally happy and sure of an admiring and responsive audience.' It emphasised how Peate had raised the profile of the club to becoming one of the best in the county: 'It was generally conceded that he retained his skill with the ball to the last and when in form his tactics were a treat which no enthusiastic cricketer could even think of missing. His presence has materially assisted the Skipton club in maintaining its position as one of the foremost exponents of the national pastime in the West Riding and his performance last season was meritorious as ever.'

Peate's reputation for dissolute behaviour followed him even in death. The *Daily Telegraph* said, 'There ought to have been many more years of good work before him but he put on weight to a great extent and in the summer of 1886 it became evident that his day was over. Without using a harsh word, it may fairly be said that he would have lasted longer if he had ordered his life more carefully.' *Wisden* continued the theme, conceding in its obituary that his career had been 'exceptionally brilliant but very short'. *Wisden's* obituary uses exactly the same wording as the *Daily Telegraph*. However, *Cricket* magazine was more charitable and put his decline down to failing eyesight rather than dropping hints.

However, both the *West Riding Pioneer* (a Skipton newspaper which was to merge with the *Craven Herald*) and the *Wharfedale Observer* both discard the disorderly lifestyle charge when they mention the sudden end to his career. They both refer to a blow to the knee from a cricket ball which meant he was no longer able to stand for three consecutive days of county cricket.

The *Wharfedale Observer* printed one of the last photographs of Peate. There is no disguising the fact that he is now of considerable bulk and a bowler hat a few sizes too small sits on his head. One cannot help but think of Oliver Hardy when he has mixed up his hat with Stan Laurel. The thick moustache is still there. Sitting with him is a dog, a mongrel type which is grey around the muzzle.

The paper reported that the dog was his constant companion and had covered thousands of miles with him on his cricket engagements.

It became clear that Peate was in straitened circumstances at the time of his death. S.R. Jackson, who had played against and alongside Peate on many occasions in his post-Yorkshire career, wrote to J.B. Wostinholm, the Yorkshire secretary, pointing out that Peate had not been given a benefit by Yorkshire and it would be most desirable if the county would do something to help the widow and children. The letter read: 'You will have noticed with regret, along with myself, the death of Mr E. Peate. I am afraid that his family will be in a very poor position for the future and, knowing that his position in Yorkshire cricket and international cricket has been of an exceptional character, it is worthy of consideration. Some time ago I suggested that Peate ought to have a benefit, which idea, unfortunately, fell to the ground to my disappointment; but seeing that he is now dead, there certainly ought to be something done for his family. It is not for me to suggest the way but to leave it to higher authorities. Yours truly, S.R. Jackson.' Yorkshire's response was that it would be more desirable if a local fund could be set up and a committee of Leeds-based gentlemen be formed to promote it.

Fortunately for Peate's dependents, there was a body of Leeds cricket supporters who were prepared to pick up the gauntlet the county club had thrown down. A public meeting was held at the Mitre Hotel in Leeds at the end of May 1900. Its purpose was to organise a fund for Peate's widow and children and was presided over by N.R. Hepworth of the Leeds Cricket, Football and Athletic Club and attended by representatives of various league and clubs with a Peate connection. Skipton and Scarborough clubs also sent in letters saying that they would hold collections and fundraising events to aid the bereaved family which was described as 'destitute'. Hepworth told the meeting that he had asked Lord Hawke if Yorkshire players could be released to play in a benefit match but was told that the rules now stipulated that the players were debarred from participating in ordinary matches during the cricket season and this could not be transgressed even for this cause. The uncompromising response is further evidence of the dictatorial and rigid rule of Hawke.

Despite this disappointment, the committee was going to press ahead with a match on Wednesday, 6 June (during Whitsuntide, a holiday week for mills and factories in many parts of Yorkshire) between teams of ex-county players and leading local players. The match was scheduled for Headingley as the Leeds CFAC had agreed to provide the ground free of charge. The Victorians could move with a rapidity we can only marvel at today and within a fortnight of this inaugural meeting of the committee the benefit match was held at Headingley on the agreed date with two members of Peate's benefit committee, Hepworth and the businessman R.S. Kirk, raising sides. Both these men had attended Peate's funeral. There was a smattering of players from Leeds and Skipton teams and an attendance put at around 2,000 paying sixpence for a ticket. The match raised £23 6 shillings and 10 pence (£23.34 in decimal currency) for the family.

The biggest boost came on 3 August when the Yorkshire committee met in Harrogate with Lord Hawke in the chair. It agreed to make a donation of £200 to the fund. This was a considerable sum – perhaps three years' salary for a skilled factory hand. Plans to try to arrange a second match after the county season had ended in which the Yorkshire players would be asked to assist were dropped. The fundraising committee heard that the Yorkshire players had already promised a donation to the fund and it was resolved to ask all clubs in the Leeds League to give the proceeds of one match, or make donations, to the fund. Other means of raising funds were to ask the county grounds and pubs in the districts to put up collection boxes.

It appears there was an attempt to keep Peate's sports shop going. The *Yorkshire Post* carried an advertisement in November 1900, eight months after his death, which stated: 'E Peate, Yorkshire County Athletic Manufactory, 8 Upper Head Row, Leeds. Billiard Cues, Cases, Tips, Wafers, Chalk etc In Stock'. There was no mention, as in the regular Peate adverts in the 1890s, of cricket and rugby equipment. It does not mean that the shop was no longer selling them but it may be that a decision had been made to concentrate on one particular sport. The advert was repeated for the last time in December 1900. In 1901 the shop was taken over by Harry Hayley, the man who had joined Peate as a professional at Headingley in 1891. Hayley was a renowned rugby player for Wakefield Trinity who also managed seven appearances for Yorkshire CCC spread over 14 years between 1884 and 1898. Peate had played alongside him in two of them. Hayley was one of those cricketers honoured by Alfred Pullin to be the subject of an interview for the *Evening Post* which was published on 18 November 1905. In it he relates how Peate had given him a severe telling-off for moving out of position when put there by the bowler. Peate had placed him at mid-off to catch Robert (R.W.) Frank, an amateur who played 18 matches for Yorkshire. The incident took place at Scarborough (according to Hayley) and a process of elimination suggests it must have been while the two were playing for Leeds. The first ball was despatched by Frank to the pavilion, so Hayley moved back from where he had been placed at mid-off to the pavilion rails. 'Next ball a half-hit went to the very place I had left,' said Hayley. 'At the end of the over, Peate came and informed me in the most eloquent language that … he thought I had enough sense to stop in the first position for the half-hit. I never disobeyed him again.' It does show that in the power dynamic, Peate was the senior professional. Hayley had been running his own sports shop, the Yorkshire County Athletic Warehouse, in Wakefield. At some point Hayley moved his Leeds business to new premises just round the corner in Queen Victoria Street and after his death in 1922 the shop was closed and stock sold off.

The total amount raised for Peate's dependents is not known. Debts would have to be cleared first but the 1901 census, taken on 31 March that year, shows that his widow Sarah had left their house in Headingley and was living in a grocer and confectioner's shop at number 23–25 in the ironically named Prosperity Street in Leeds, a series of back-to-back houses. The children were now 19 and 17 years old and the youngest, Lizzie, is shown as working as a confectioner in her mother's shop. Edmund described himself as a plumber. So it seems that the fund had set up Sarah Peate with the means of making a living.

By the time of the next census in 1911, Peate's children had both fled the nest to leave Sarah running the shop on her own. It must have been a struggle and, as so often before, the pull of Yeadon was too strong. She had returned there by 1921 and at the age of 63 was working as a burler and winder (the same job she had after her marriage 40 years previously) at J.J.&C. Peate and Co Ltd in Nunroyd Mills in Yeadon. The Peate she was now working for was no relative of Ted's. This was Jonathan Peate, who had risen from humble beginnings to start his own textile business, building Nunroyd Mill in partnership with his brothers Joseph and Caleb. The mill is now demolished and covered by a retail park. Sarah died at the age of 69 in 1927.

Edmund junior left West Yorkshire sometime before the 1911 census where he is recorded as living in Denaby, near

Doncaster, where he was working in the mines as a surface coal inspector. He had spent some years in Macclesfield where he was married to Mary Ellen. His eldest son, also named Edmund after his famous grandfather, was born in Macclesfield but a second boy, George, was born in Denaby in 1910. Peate's son died aged 92 in Pontefract in 1974. Peate's daughter Lizzie left her mother's sweet shop in 1908 to marry Charles Herbert Knight, a sorting clerk and telegraphist, who was from Barnsley. The couple were living here in 1911, about ten miles away from her brother, and they had at least two children, Catherine and James. Lizzie Peate died in 1975 in Leeds.

Ted's proud collection of cricket mementoes has disappeared. A cricket box, with his name stencilled on the side, is in the Headingley museum but the mounted balls, walking sticks and cigarette cases he so proudly displayed to journalist Alfred Pullin in 1897 are no longer in the family. Nor is the illuminated address presented to him by Yeadon Cricket Club. His great grandson, John, recalls playing with the memorabilia as a child but no-one now knows where they ended up.

The benefit fund saved Sarah Peate and her children from the workhouse. It did not stretch to a headstone for Ted's grave. As planes take off from the runway at Leeds-Bradford airport a glance down to the left provides a view of Yeadon cemetery. There, in an unmarked grave, section A plot 241, lie the remains of one of England's finest spin bowlers.

Ted Peate's Career Statistics

BOWLING

	Balls	Mdns	Runs	Wkts	Best	Ave	5wkt	10wkt
Overall	47025	5667	14517	1076	8-5	13.49	94	27
Test matches	2096	250	683	31	6-85	22.03	2	0
Season by season								
1879	2744	293	933	75	6-14	12.44	9	4
1880	5182	579	1662	138	8-24	12.04	13	5
1881	6851	760	2196	173	8-30	12.69	14	3
1881/82 (Australia)	1979	234	553	30	6-30	18.43	2	0
1882	7449	866	2466	214	8-32	11.52	21	8
1883	5505	665	1753	120	8-5	14.60	10	2
1884	6260	788	1868	137	8-63	13.63	13	3
1885	6804	903	1945	115	6-17	16.91	8	1
1886	3922	540	1027	70	8-23	14.67	4	1
1887	234	32	70	2	1-26	35.00	0	0
1890	95	7	44	2	1-22	22.00	0	0

BATTING

	Matches	Innings	Not out	Runs	Highest	Average
Overall	209	312	88	2384	95	10.64
Test matches	9	14	8	70	13	11.66
Season by season						
1879	15	21	5	50	23	3.12
1880	22	32	13	142	27*	7.47
1881	26	36	20	159	28*	9.93
1881/82 (Australia)	7	13	7	104	33*	17.33
1882	30	45	6	429	48	11.00
1883	27	40	6	406	61	11.94
1884	30	47	10	510	95	13.78
1885	29	40	10	367	39	12.23
1886	20	32	10	189	30	8.59
1887	2	4	1	14	11*	4.66
1890	1	2	0	14	13	7.00

Acknowledgements

DEDICATED TO the late Ted Peate, who has been maligned for far too long.

The late Keith Handley was the first to recognise that Ted Peate's reputation needed rehabilitating and was the first to attempt a biography. Alas he died before his project was completed and his research did not survive him.

I am grateful to many people who gave their time to help with this book.

Two members of the Association of Cricket Statisticians, Brian Sanderson and Rodney Ulyate, gave me advice and chewed over a few opinions with me. They pointed me in the right direction and probably prevented me from making the odd howler.

Others too were only too willing to offer their assistance in helping with my research and for this I am eternally grateful. They include, in no particular order:

John Dewhirst, whose outstanding research into the origins of football clubs Bradford City and Bradford Park Avenue was always an inspiration and an example to follow.

Myffanwy Bryant of the Australian National Maritime Museum, who gave valuable assistance from afar supplying documents on the *Chimborazo* passenger ship bringing Peate home from the Australian tour.

James Philip, for his thoughts and input following his late father's monograph on Billy Brockwell.

The staff at the Local and Family History Library, based at Leeds library, were patient and helpful in tracking down the location of Ted's shop on The Headrow and confirming a few details of his Leeds addresses.

Similarly tolerant were the staff at Skipton library for making available reports from the local papers of Peate's time at Skipton.

Jai Mukherjee and officials at Skipton Cricket Club allowed me to peruse whatever artefacts the club still possesses from the Peate era.

Members of Aireborough History Society kindly provided a flavour of the Yeadon of Peate's childhood and clarified a few details about locations.

Thanks to Dave Robinson of Skipton, a Yorkshire CCC supporter who gave me the kick up the backside to stop talking about the book and start writing it.

Thanks also to Pitch Publishing for having the foresight to publish a biography of the great Ted Peate.

Finally, thanks to my wife Shan who, without complaint, put up with sharing our lives with Ted Peate.

Bibliography

Birley, Derek – *A Social History of English Cricket* (Aurum Press, 2003)

Briggs, Simon – *Stiff Upper Lips and Baggy Green Caps: A Sledger's History of the Ashes* (Quercus, 2013)

Coldham, James – *Lord Hawke, a cricketing biography* (Crowood Press, 1990)

Coldham, James – *William Brockwell: His Triumph and Tragedy*. Kindle Edition

Hodgson, Derek – *The Official History of Yorkshire County Cricket Club* (Crowood Press, 1989)

Holmes, Rev. R.S. – *The History of Yorkshire County Cricket Club 1833–1903* (Archibald Constable, 1904)

Kelly's Leeds Directory (years from 1890 to 1901)

Light, Rob – 'Ten Drunks and a Parson? The Victorian Professional Cricketer Reconsidered'; *Sport in History* vol 25 issue 1 (2005)

Melville, Tom – *The Tented Field, A History of Cricket in America* (University of Wisconsin Press, 1998)

Pollard, Jack – *The Formative Years of Australian Cricket 1803–93* (Angus & Robertson, 1987)

Pullin, Alfred – *Talks with Old English Cricketers* (Blackwood & Sons, 1900)

Ranjitsinhji, KS – *The Jubilee Book of Cricket* (1897) viewed online at https://en.wikisource.org/wiki/The_Jubilee_Book_of_Cricket

Sandford, Keith – 'Amateurs and Professionals in Victorian County Cricket' published in *Albion*: A quarterly journal of British studies vol 15 issue 1 (1983)

Sissons, RIC – *The Players, a Social History of the Professional Cricketer* (Kingswood Press, 1988)

Slater, Philomen – *The History of the Ancient Parish of Guiseley* (1880)

Thomas, Peter – *Yorkshire Cricketers 1839–1939* (reprinted Derek Hodgson, 1973)

Ulyate, Rodney – *The Autobiography of Edward Pooley* (Independently published, 2023)

Vamplew, Wray – 'Alcohol and the Sportsperson'; *Sport in History* vol 25, issue 3 (2005)

Whitehead, Richard (edit) – *The Times on the Ashes* (The History Press, 2015)

Wilde, Simon – *The Tour: The Story of the England Cricket Team Overseas 1877–2023* (Simon and Schuster, 2023)

Wisden on the Ashes (edited Steve Lynch) – John Wisden (2009)

Wisden on Yorkshire (edited Duncan Hamilton) – John Wisden (2011)

Woodhouse, Anthony – *The History of Yorkshire County Cricket Club* (Helm publishers, 1989)

For article on 1882 scandal https://oldebor.wordpress.com/2021/09/08/whatever-the-scheme-actually-was-it-failed-match-fixing-denials-and-cover-ups/
For all cricket statistics www.cricketarchive.com (subscription required)

Magazines and periodicals consulted (most available via subscription at www.britishnewspaperarchive.co.uk):

Athletic News
Bradford Observer
Carlisle Patriot

Craven Herald
Cricket Magazine
Daily Telegraph
Huddersfield Daily Examiner
Leeds Daily News
Manchester Guardian
Sheffield Telegraph
Southern Daily News
Sporting Times
The Magnet
The Sportsman
West Sussex Journal
West Yorkshire Pioneer
Wharfedale Observer
Yorkshire Post
Yorkshire Evening Post
Yorkshire Evening Press

Australian newspapers available via https://trove.nla.
gov.au/newspaper